A Different Jesus

A CHRISTIAN THEOLOGY BIG ENOUGH FOR AN INTERFAITH WORLD

by Jan G. Linn

This is the first book of three in the series:
A Christianity Big Enough for the World

ISBN 10: 1-59152-144-0
ISBN 13: 978-1-59152-144-0

Biblical quotations, unless otherwise noted, are from the New Revised Standard Version Bible, copyright 1989, Division of Christian Education of the National Council of Churches in the United States of America.

For other books by Jan G. Linn, visit Amazon.com.

You may order extra copies of this book by calling Farcountry Press toll free at (800) 821-3874.

s**weetgrass**books
a division of Farcountry Press

Produced by Sweetgrass Books.
PO Box 5630, Helena, MT 59604; (800) 821-3874; www.sweetgrassbooks.com.

Printed in the United States of America.

18 17 16 15 14   1 2 3 4 5

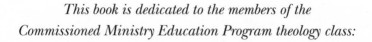

This book is dedicated to the members of the
Commissioned Ministry Education Program theology class:

Russell Alexander
Dennis Arnold
Marsha Borders
Gary Brooks
Jenny Butler Curnes
David Dunahoo
Don Embree

Bruce Gowen
Donna Gustafson
Willa Heaberlin
Bob Merkley
Pat Stalter
Heather Wachendorf
Clinton Wallace

And their instructor: Bryan Feille, Ph.D.

Reflecting on the class experience, Dr. Feille commented:

"Jan's book provoked thought and discussion. Based on a lifetime of reflecting on the meaning of Jesus, he challenges conventional, unreflective understandings of Jesus. Some students honestly struggled and were compelled to rethink their own beliefs. Others found Jan to be one who gave voice to their faith. I will continue to use the book in groups that are serious in thinking about their faith."

*"All I can do is to try to be honest—
honest to God and honest about God—
and to follow the argument
wherever it leads."*

—*Honest to God,*[1] *Bishop John A. T. Robinson*

❧ CONTENTS ❧

Acknowledgments 6

A Personal Statement of Faith 7

Chapter 1
Honest Faith 13

Chapter 2
In the Beginning God 17

Chapter 3
Images of God Matter 21

Chapter 4
Jewish Roots of Christian Atonement 31

Chapter 5
Jesus and the Salvation of Christians 43

Chapter 6
Resurrection Salvation 49

Chapter 7
Jesus and the Kingdom of God 63

Chapter 8
Heaven, Hell, the Ascension, and the
       Second Coming of Jesus 75

Chapter 9
A Jesus to Believe In 87

Endnotes 97

✦ ACKNOWLEDGMENTS ✦

Several people read this book in its early stages and made invaluable suggestions for improvements. My sincere gratitude to Bill Blackwell, Loren Olson, Ron Roberts, Charlie Curry, Bob and Monica Hatch, Ivan Lyddon, Craig Watts, Garry Hesser, the members of the Commissioned Ministry Education Program theology class* (to whom the book is dedicated), and especially to Tamara Rodenberg, Jeff Slade, Luke Lindon, and Bryan Feille.

I also want to thank my wife, Joy, for reading countless versions of this material over a three-year period, encouraging me to finish the work, and making so many helpful suggestions that for all practical purposes this work is as much hers as mine.

Finally, this book was born of numerous conversations I had over many years with church members, church dropouts, and people who do not consider themselves religious or spiritual but who have an intellectual interest in religious questions, all of whom could not make sense of Christianity's exclusive claims to truth that left all non-Christians "behind." What I realized over time is that their issues with the Christian faith came down to not being able to understand why a good God would require the death of "his son" (their words) in order to forgive them of their sins. This book is my response to their struggle.

*The Commissioned Ministry Educational Program is a ministry
of the Christian Church (Disciples of Christ) in the Upper Midwest.

A PERSONAL STATEMENT OF FAITH

This book is written for Christians who believe in Jesus but have serious questions about the meaning of his being the savior of the world. They want to be Christian without believing that God rejects everyone who is not. Ironically, surveys suggest these Christians are actually a majority now, but they don't know that.[2] Consequently they feel out of place in the church. Many of them have dropped out. Others are hanging on by a thin thread.

I hope this book will help these individuals see that it's possible to be thoroughly Christian without dismissing or condemning all other religions. I also hope this material will help those who *do* believe Jesus is the *only* way to better understand those of us who don't.

I did not come to believe in Jesus as a way to God—but not the only way—overnight. I was raised in a large, conservative church that not only told me Jesus was the only way, but also that the Bible was literally the Word of God (meaning the King James Version). The people in my home church loved and supported me as a child of the congregation and later as a student studying for the ministry. But there came a point where I knew that what they taught me was no longer what I believed, not because I doubted my own faith, but because I doubted what they taught me about theirs.

Anyone who has been in that situation knows how emotionally stressful it can be. A sense of separation builds between you and the people you love the most. That was happening to me until I spent a week with my hometown minister, who was holding a preaching mission at the student church I was serving. He was a dynamic but humble minister loved by the entire city as well as our congregation. Even though his theology was more conservative than mine had become, as the week progressed I began to see that he genuinely believed in what he said. More than that, I knew him well enough to know that the goal of his life was to serve God. At the end of the week, I admired him even more than I had before. We were no closer theologically, but I realized that what mattered more than theology was our relationship.

That is a lesson I have drawn on many times in my ministry, in part because I have found myself at theological odds with a variety of people for a variety of reasons. It is not because I enjoy conflict. I don't. It is because I think that what we believe as Christians is too important to merely accept claims on blind faith. Moreover, I believe wrestling with questions is vital to spiritual growth. It is a primary way many of us who are Christian make faith our own.

At the center of my questions is, of course, Jesus. Who was he really? Was he human and divine? What does that even mean? Did he die for the sins of the world? If so, how can people of other faith traditions who are friends of mine be in a relationship with God if they don't believe in Jesus? What is the core of Christian belief? Or, in other words, is there any single belief without which the entire house of cards would come tumbling down?

This book is my answer to those questions. By the time you finish reading, I hope you will see why I believe Jesus was the man he was and why it was God raising him from the dead rather than his crucifixion that changed the world, opening the door to a faith that can thrive in the religiously plural nation that is the United States today.

But I am getting ahead of myself. I realize that the waters of Christian belief run deep, and emotions attached to faith can be so strong that they overwhelm our capacity to think through what someone who is challenging long-standing beliefs is actually saying. This happens to all of us. For this reason I want to underscore that my intention in writing this book is to build up faith, not tear it down. I want to strengthen the church's witness, not undermine it.

At the same time, when dealing with an existing structure, construction necessarily involves some deconstruction. This is as true for beliefs as it is for actual buildings. Thus, deconstructing or unlearning things we were taught to believe and/or still believe is an unavoidable part of constructing a different content to our faith. Moreover, because the church has taught many things that need to be reexamined, there is a lot of deconstruction work to do.

Unfortunately, what some Christians believe about the Bible works against them when they experience deconstruction. Literalism, or believing every word in the Bible was dictated by God, has led some people to view questions regarding traditional beliefs in a negative way. Sadly, it has also instilled in them a fear that if what they think the Bible says isn't true, their faith is in vain.

Part of the problem literalism creates is that it blurs the distinction between reading the Bible historically and reading it devotionally. The former tries to discover what the biblical writers meant when they wrote what they wrote. The latter is what a text or book means to an individual personally. Both ways of reading the Bible are important, but also different. Literalism ignores that difference.

Biblical literalism also tends to ignore the fact that Christian beliefs and the Christian community itself existed well into the fourth century before anything close to what we call the Christian Bible was completed and widely accepted. Even then, because of the hundreds of biblical texts in circulation, questions about which books should be in the Bible and which should not continued for centuries. Add to this the fact that no original biblical manuscripts exist today, only copies, and also hundreds of imperfect translations available to the public, it is easy to see why for many people biblical literalism has been a hindrance to spiritual growth and development, rather than a help.

My approach here is markedly different from biblical literalism, and is one that I believe makes the biblical message much more accessible to us today than literalism does. This method is to understand the Bible as story. Not a fairy-tale type of story, but a story akin to a testimonial that describes what someone has seen and experienced. The Bible is a testimony—a story—that begins with creation, recounts the divine/human relationship through the people called Israel, and focuses on a man named Jesus who captured the imagination and hearts of his own people; it ends with his story turning the non-Jewish world upside down, just as it had among the Jews of his day.

The Bible is composed of the many stories that people of faith told through the centuries, which have endured because one generation after another has claimed the truth of those stories for themselves. In the truest sense the Bible is our story as well as theirs. History is to be found in the stories, but history is not the point. Identity is. Knowing who we are and what we are meant to do in the world because of who we are is the point.

Once we claim the Bible as story for ourselves, theology becomes the particular way in which we tell that story so that it describes who we are as people of faith. In this way theology becomes a witness to what we believe and why. This is how we connect to the Bible. Its story becomes ours, and then our own story informs how we understand the story of those who have gone before us.

The material that follows falls into the category of story. It is a testimony of my faith that is grounded in the story of scripture and my own life experiences. It is not doctrine or dogma. It is a simple witness to what I have come to believe is true about the Jesus whose path I follow as a way to do the will of God. As you will see, what I believe about Jesus allows me to follow him while also including non-Christians among the people of God.

At the same time, I realize that saying something like this can generate strong negative feelings among people who believe Jesus is the *only* way to God. If you are one of them, you will probably feel yourself being stretched in uncomfortable ways as you read. I can only ask that you persevere and withhold final judgment until you have read the entire book.

If, on the other hand, what you find in these pages is an

expression of faith that connects with where you are spiritually, I hope reading the book gives you good reason to believe you can be Christian and also have a faith that takes seriously the reality of living in today's religiously plural world.

Finally, as a Christian I believe there is ultimate "truth," but it is a truth that is beyond our reach. None of us, therefore, knows the truth absolutely. At the end of the day, I believe the best any of us can do is to tell all the truth we know without claiming to know all the truth there is. After that we can and must trust ourselves to the love and grace of God.

CHAPTER ONE

Honest Faith

ORRIS SHAPIRO WAS the rabbi of a Reform congregation in my hometown. Having observed his amazing language skills (he could read Hebrew as well as I could read English), I asked if he would help me improve my ability to read Hebrew scripture. He agreed, and through the years we became the best of friends. But it was his spirit of grace and openness that drew me to him. He was a man of deep faith and incredible generosity. We exchanged pulpits between the synagogue he led and the college chapel where I served as chaplain. I celebrated holy days with his congregation. We were brothers in the faith, even though he was a Jew and I was a Christian. Years later I mourned his death, and thought to myself that I would not want to go to heaven if it had no place for Morris Shapiro.

Khaled Elabdi, a native of Morocco, is a Sufi Muslim who teaches English as a second language in our local school system. My first encounter came when I called to ask if he would speak about Islam to the congregation my wife and I were serving as co-pastors. He responded by inviting us to his home for the Friday meal that would mark the breaking of the Ramadan fast. He and his wife, Theresa, an American he met while she was serving in Morocco as a Peace Corps volunteer, were gracious hosts. As the evening came to a close, I asked him if he had any specific hopes for the three lectures he had agreed to deliver. His answer was simple. "A friendship," he said. "I would like this to be the beginning of a friendship between us." To my great joy, it was.

Morris Shapiro was and Khaled Elabdi is a man of God. Our friendships connected with the inner stirrings in my heart, which for many years had been nudging me to grow my faith big enough to follow Jesus without needing to believe he was the only way to God. Indeed, it is precisely because I follow Jesus that I don't believe that, and why I do believe Morris Shapiro and Khaled Elabdi are enveloped by the grace of God, as I am. For any Christian to believe they are not saddens me greatly. At times it makes me angry. Christianity is too important to the world to be left to people who think this way. But it is the church that must share part of the blame for this kind of thinking and should also bear the responsibility for doing something about it. Christians can be bigger and better than triumphal Christianity. Jesus certainly was, and God certainly is. The least we can do is be honest enough with ourselves to admit that we have made serious theological mistakes that need to be corrected.

THE NATURE OF FAITH

Core to expanding our theological perspective is to understand what having faith means. In the first place, faith is not something one person can impose on another. "Those who believe, believe; those who don't, don't," observes Amy-Jill Levine and Douglas Knight, both seminary professors at Vanderbilt, the former Jewish, the latter Christian. "Belief is like love," they go on to say. "It cannot be compelled; it does not function on logical parameters. As some religions would put it, faith is a matter of 'grace.' For these traditions, we do not summon faith; it summons us."[3]

Moreover, having faith is not the same thing as knowing facts. Faith needs to take facts seriously, but it also goes beyond facts and reaches conclusions the world cannot or will not reach. If you have facts, you don't need faith. If you have faith you need facts, but you also need more than facts. You need courage to ultimately believe what facts cannot tell you is true. A problem arises, however, when people are careless about distinguishing faith from facts. They make a faith statement as if it is an established fact, when in reality it is a conclusion reached through faith.

Many Christians are tempted to do that. They might say, for example, "Jesus died for our sins," without thinking that while this may be true, it may also not be true. The same can be said of the fundamental claim that God is real. It may or may not be true. These are statements of faith, not fact. That is the nature of all faith claims. They may contain facts, but are not facts themselves. Indeed, we know that people believe many things that turn out not to be true. Having faith is not in itself a reason for anyone else to consider what we believe to be true.

Yet faith is an essential tool of human existence in all areas of life. Despite the fact that "faith" literally means "belief that is not based on proof," it is something that allows us to function in life. A husband or wife trusts the fidelity of the other without proof of it, or even asking for it. Drivers trust the competence and sensibleness of every other driver on the road. Passengers flying to a holiday in the Bahamas trust the pilot is competent. Faith is employed every day by everyone. It is something no one can live without.

There are, of course, numerous occasions when faith is betrayed. A wife finds out her husband has been having an affair with a coworker. A faithful husband discovers when he comes home from a job he hates that his wife has packed up and left. Pilots have been known to drink on the job. Drivers talking on cell phones cause accidents. Companies fire aging employees who were trusting them to do the right thing. Employers find out some workers have been sabotaging their business because of anger or meanness.

On the face of it, the fact that people have faith is a rather ordinary thing. Religious faith is simply another dimension of how all people live—believing something without proof of it. Matters of faith don't lend themselves to certainty; otherwise, they would not be expressions of faith. I may say, for example, that God is concerned about the poor. I believe this because it is a central tenet in the Christian Bible. It is not actually a fact, though. It is a conjecture of faith, which for me is enough.

Guarding against making faith assertions into statements of absolute truth is critically important for Christians to bear in mind. Once you make this mistake, it is tempting to take the next step and insist that your perception of truth is a necessary truth for everyone. You may even feel free, if not obligated, to make judgments about the fate of those who refuse to accept your version of truth.

When Christians think and believe this way, they fall into the trap of forgetting that the very nature of faith is that what we believe can be right and it can also be wrong. This is because faith is not about facts. Facts lead to conclusions based on known evidence, which can change only when new evidence is uncovered. Faith doesn't live by facts. It doesn't wait until all the facts are known. It chooses to live by what it "sees" through the lens of belief. It is important that every person of faith understands that this is what having faith means.

CHAPTER TWO

In the Beginning God

ONCE YOU UNDERSTAND the nature of faith, you are ready to do theology. Yet the word "theology" may sound intimidating. You may think it is a subject too deep for you to understand or is another name for undermining faith. Whatever you may think when you hear the word "theology," rest assured it is something you and everyone around you engages in all the time.

The word has a simple meaning—thinking about God. That is what "study" involves, thinking. So when a theologian "studies" God, she is thinking about God in an effort to understand what believing in God means. Everyone who believes in God thinks about God, some more than others. Even people who don't believe in God think about God. It is not an exaggeration to say that theology is something we do because we are human. As such it is natural and can be efficacious, and is certainly not something to be feared or avoided. If anything, theology, or thinking about God, needs more attention rather than less.

A CHURCH WITHOUT ALL THE ANSWERS

The outspoken Benedictine writer Sister Joan Chittister has said:

If there is one thing that we have been taught to fear, it is surely questions. There are some things, we learn early, that are never to be challenged. They simply are. They are absolute. They come out of a fountain of eternal truth. And they are true because someone else said they are true. So we live with someone else's answers for a long time. Until the answers run dry. I know that because I myself have been caught in the desert of doubt and found the answers to be worse than the questions could ever be.[4]

Many Christians understand exactly what Joan Chittister is talking about. Their experience in church has been anything but a chance to seek truth. Many of them have already left church, convinced that they cannot be the kind of Christian they want to be and remain. They are Christians who value honest inquiry. They welcome guidance, but will not be told what to believe or how to think. Congregations that want to attract them back to church will see theological education as one of their primary tasks.

Churches would do well, then, to understand that encouraging theological inquiry is more important than giving answers. The goal should not be conformity of belief but mature faith, faith that can stand on its own legs and speak from its own heart. The need for this kind of faith has never been more acute. Congregations that encourage fresh thinking rather than holding firm to accepted doctrine and dogma are, I believe, where the future lies. There really is no need for any Christian or any church to be afraid of the pursuit of truth. It is the road to spiritual freedom.

THE CHOICE FOR GOD

The biblical writer understood the starting point of faith when he wrote: "In the Beginning God . . ." (Genesis 1:1). God is where everything begins. Nothing a person of faith believes matters if God doesn't exist. I think one of the ironies of church history is that Christians have engaged in bitter debate about the nature of Jesus without paying much attention to the more basic question: "Does God exist?" But if we are serious about having a theology big enough for the world, this is where we must begin.

As a pastor I have faced situations where I wished I could prove to a church member that God is real. Parents of a child battling cancer would be comforted by such proof. So would a young man going off to war, a single mother of three facing cancer surgery, a family of unemployed parents wondering if they are going to lose their home. Pastors are constantly asking their church members to pray for people in need, to attend worship regularly, and to help people who need the basic necessities of life, because these are the things God expects of them. But every challenge rests on the fundamental assumption that God is real. Believing God is real is the most profound choice a person makes in life. Nothing else equals its impact. To believe in God or not to believe in God is literally a life-changing decision.

What I want to underscore is that belief in God is a choice. I have been asked on numerous occasions by a wide range of people why I believe in God. My answer is always the same. It is a choice I have made. Strong emotions are attached to this choice because of personal experiences that I attribute to the presence and watch-care of God. I am a minister, for example, because I felt called by God when I was in college. That moment remains vivid in my memory and, in fact, has sustained me all these years, especially during difficult times. But at bottom I understand that what I believe was a call to ministry and my believing in God at all were choices I made and continue to make. That is the nature of faith. If I knew for a fact that God existed, or didn't exist, it would be foolish to believe otherwise. But no such certainty exists. The essence of faith is to choose belief over non-belief.

One of the practical implications of the decision to believe in God is that we are acknowledging we are not God, the consequence of which is the realization that our life is no longer our own to do with as we please. At that point our life's goal becomes what the Apostle Paul says it is for people of faith—to live a life that is well pleasing to God (Romans 12:2). He is saying that believing in God means trying to do with your life what you best understand God's will to be. It is easy, then, to see why believing in God is a profound decision to make. If I choose not to believe in God, I am free to please myself. If I believe in God, I have chosen to try to live a life that pleases God.

But is there any reason to believe in God? Scholars such as scientist Richard Dawkins and philosopher Sam Harris say "no." At the opposite end of the spectrum, American physician-geneticist Francis Collins, former director of the National Institutes of Health, says "yes," as do Jewish, Christian, and Islamic scholars around the world. It does come down to a matter of perspective, but believing in God does not have to be pitted against scientific discovery, as some would argue.

To a large extent, arguments made for and against the existence of God make sense to those making them, while sounding unconvincing to those who disagree. No one believes in God's existence solely on the basis of evidence, but the same is true for those rejecting God's existence. As strange as it may sound, both are decisions of faith, even though those who make the argument against God may refuse to acknowledge it, convinced as they are that there is no evidence of God. But in logic you cannot prove a negative, so the nonexistence of God cannot be proven. Atheists, therefore, are simply choosing not to believe, while people of faith are making a different choice.[5]

CHAPTER THREE

Images of God Matter

Faith in God, then, is always a choice, making the entire debate about the existence of God fruitless. At the same time, the particular ways in which all of us think about God, or the kind of image of God we carry around in our head, matters a great deal.

I realize that images of God are a sensitive subject. People hold certain beliefs because they find solace and comfort in them. At the same time, biblical writers did not view images of God as inconsequential. The Torah prohibited the use of idols precisely because Israel believed physical images would represent an attempt to capture the essence of God who can never be fully known (Exodus 20:1-4).

This prohibition might well apply to our own conceptions of God. How you or I conceive of God is important because words represent a particular understanding of God. In addition, it is important to remember that God is not limited by what either of us says about God. Images of God matter, not because they capture who God is, but because they can have a significant impact on the way we act and on the way others perceive and respond to God. In short, images of God are anything but benign.

That said, scripture is not always as helpful as we would like when speaking of God since, as Amy-Jill Levine and Douglas Knight note, scripture does not provide any single image of God that is definitive. "The Bible...refuses a singular picture of the Deity, which means that no individual rabbi or priest or pastor can claim complete theological knowledge. The biblical text is an anthology, with different perspectives given of the Deity and with different names."

Yet for Christians there is one source for an image of God that takes precedent over all others. It is the God we believe was made known in Jesus. That is the image we are after here. But to get there we first need to evaluate troublesome images of God that sharply contrast the one we believe Jesus revealed. Each separately and all of them together underscore the need for caution when speaking about God.

GOD AS INTERVENER

The picture of former Denver Bronco quarterback Tim Tebow down on one knee praying during ball games during the 2011 season was etched into the memory of viewers nationwide. The action became known as "Tebowing." Tebow said he wasn't praying for God to help his team win, but the public perception said otherwise. Months later several of the track and field stars who won a race that put them on the 2012 U.S. Olympic team made comments that suggested a similar message. They attributed their wins to trusting in God. One went so far as to say she had prayed and prayed for God to give her the strength to run the race of her life, which she did. That night I watched an HBO boxing match. The winner began his after fight interview saying he wanted to "give all praise to God" for giving him the strength to win the fight. Months later the first thing a winner on the PGA Tour said on the eighteenth green was, "I just have to thank my Lord and Savior, Jesus Christ, for giving me the strength and ability to be here."

Not everyone who believes God intervenes in their lives agrees with these kinds of comments, but I think it is fair to say that each example reflects how difficult it is to limit how God intervenes in life once you start down that road. Moreover, while we may be inclined to think these athletes are simply expressing their thanksgiving to God for the good thing that happened to them, the public perception of their words and/or actions says much more than that. Whatever explanation Tim Tebow gave for his bended knee pose, the audience believed he was praying for victory. And why wouldn't they? Before the 2014 Super Bowl a survey by the Public Religion Research Institute in Washington, D.C. found that as many as 70 million Americans believed God or the supernatural would be at work in the game's outcome. The survey also said that half of sports fans believe that their team can be cursed and that well-behaved players are blessed. Thirty-eight percent of white evangelical Protestants say they often ask God to help their team.

The idea that God cares about athletic events of any kind, especially ones involving highly paid players or violence such as what happens in a boxing match, presents an image of God as One who makes arbitrary decisions about who to help and who not to help. It is easy to dismiss the boxer who thanks God for knocking out his opponent as naïve or misguided, but the image of God is the same in all such instances. God helps some, but not others, cares about trivial matters like a game while ignoring storms that destroy lives and property.

The idea that God would care about a game, but doesn't intervene to heal a dying child whose prayers have been constant pushes the limit of any credibility God's goodness has for the reason I noted earlier. Saying one event is because of the hand of God, but rejecting another creates confusion and makes God seem capricious, if not uncaring. It seems to me the prudent thing would be to move with extreme caution when speaking about God's role in specific moments in our lives, leaving the good that comes to one person and the bad to another to mystery rather than falling to the temptation to explain either one.

GOD AS PUNISHER

As troublesome as the image of God as Intervener is, God as Punisher raises even more obstacles for credibility.

The debate before honor students at a local high school in which I spoke against a proposed amendment to our state Constitution that would ban gay marriage had just ended when one of the students approached me to ask a question. "Don't you believe in a God of justice?" she asked. I responded that I believed in a God of grace and love, to which she replied, "I know God is an awesome God who loves me in amazing ways, but God is also a just God who has to punish us for our sins because justice demands it."

Those who believe in God as Punisher tend to be confident the Bible speaks of God in this way. At a very elementary level you can understand why they would think this way. The Book of Deuteronomy, for example, says God would reward the Hebrew people if they were faithful in the new land, but would punish them if they were not. Not surprisingly, the Bible also says just the opposite. The Book of Job directly challenges the Deuteronomic image of God as Punisher. It goes even further in insisting this image of God is wrong. In truth the image of God presented in each book, and in all the books of the Bible, is based on beliefs held by the writer and conditioned by the times in which the book was written. These views help us to think about the kind of God we believe in, but they are not binding on how we understand God today.

More than anything, though, the image of God as One who rewards and punishes contradicts the way of unconditional love so evident in the ministry of Jesus. If punishment is the consequence of not following the will of God, there is, then, no unconditional love on the part of God and no freedom of choice for humanity. This is the fundamental problem with this image of God. As parents we want our children to be good and do good, but once we have taught them how to make those choices, they must be free to do so. But if they always stand in danger of losing our love, or being punished for going against our will for their lives, they are kept as children and never allowed to grow up.

The same is true in the divine/human relationship. In order to love God freely, we have been given freedom of choice by God who loves us unconditionally. There are consequences, of course, for the decisions we make, but they are ones we bring on ourselves rather than being caused by God. Thus, we really do reap what we sow, which the Apostle Paul said was the way of God (Galatians 6:7). Here is where those who believe in God as Punisher get confused. They associate good and bad with God rather than the way life functions. They ignore the fact that innocent people suffer, while bad people prosper. This is what the Book of Job says unequivocally, in contradistinction to Deuteronomy. This is the way life is, not the way God responds to what we do and don't do.

Here, again, it is difficult to see how God as Punisher can escape the negative image of God it represents, offering no incentive to being better or doing better at following God's will than we do. It is, instead, an ancient worldview of the ways of God that is too small for the world we live in. Human beings bear responsibility for the decisions we make and consequences those decisions produce. God is neither the cause of nor shoulders the blame for those consequences.

GOD AS CONTROLLER

It is often the case that someone who believes in God as Intervener will also believe in God as Punisher, each rooted in the image of God as Controller.

Some Christians say they believe God has a plan for their lives. On the other hand, experience suggests few live as if this is actually true. The belief in a divine meta-plan for our lives is one of those assertions that leads to the conclusion that your life is not really your own, but is being controlled by God. While this image of a God may offer comfort to some people, I personally cannot understand why it does or why anyone thinks it would to a grieving family.

Journalist E. J. Montini whose columns appear in the Arizona Republic wrote about a high school student who died as a result of a head injury while playing football. An anonymous reader wrote to him to say, "What happened to this young man could have happened to him in any sport. This story has more to do with the fact that when it's your time, it's your time, than it does with football."

I supposed this image of God was behind the comment a person made on FaceBook after a 16 year old high school student in our area was killed in a car accident. "God had other plans," she wrote, "and now she stands in his presence, a heavenly angel to all of us. What a beautiful place for her to be." Sadly, people who make these kinds of statement have not thought through the full implications of what they are saying. A man survives a harrowing experience and says he guesses it just wasn't his time; a woman survives cancer surgery and concludes God must still have more for her to do, a child dies and a neighbor says God must have needed her in heaven, these may have the intention of bringing comfort or hope, but when reflected on carefully end up making a bad situation worse.

Yet books that promote the image of God as Intervener, Controller or Punisher are often quite popular. Well known pastor Rick Warren's of a few years ago, *The Purpose Driven Life*, is a case in point. He argued that God has a plan for everyone's life each of us must follow if we are to live the life we were intended to live. Seems like a reasonable thing to believe so long as it remains vague and general. Indeed, I think it is a good thing to believe God wants nothing but good for our lives. But to go the next step and say that what happens in your life or mine is part of a divine plan creates more problems than any comfort it might bring.

We can bring meaning out of bad circumstances, but that is not the same thing as saying God intended those bad things to happen. Bad things do in fact happen, and to good people.

But the opposite is also true. Good things happen, and sometimes to bad people. It is part of the randomness of life over which we have some control and for which we bear more than our share of responsibility.

GOD AS LOVE

Images of God matter, then, because they have the potential of enhancing or diminishing both faith and life. The ones already discussed are but three of many that when carried to their logical conclusion become a barrier to the concept of God as good. Yet, as we have acknowledged, scripture contains no single and unified image of God. So what do we do? Perhaps we should do what Christians usually do to understand God better. We look to Jesus. We look at his life and listen to his words to see if he revealed a dominant image of God.

When we do we quickly arrive at what seems to me to be a universally held belief that the primary image revealed in the person of Jesus is that God is love. Jesus speaks of God as "Abba," not one to be feared, but loved as a daughter loves her father. This God surprises us by inviting the most unlikely among us to the table and questions the presumption of those who want to exclude us. This God is merciful and gracious, a God whose love is the reason the Apostle Paul wrote poetically about love being "patient . . . kind . . . not envious or boastful or arrogant or rude . . . does not insist on its own way . . . is not irritable or resentful . . . does not rejoice in wrongdoing, but rejoices in the truth . . . [and] bears all things, believes all things, hopes all things, endures all things (1 Corinthian 13:4-7)."

This image of God speaks of a divine love that is unconditional, unrestrained, and unrestricted, even shocking and scandalous in the degree to which it goes to reach out to a desperate humanity. The writer of the First Letter of John declares, "Beloved, let us love one another, because love is from God; everyone who loves is born of God and knows God" (1 John 4:7). This is an image of God to be trusted.

To reinforce the image of a loving and gracious God Jesus told a parable of a wayward son who is welcomed home by his father after squandering his inheritance in foolish living. It is a familiar parable we call the Parable of the Prodigal Son (Luke 15:11-32), perhaps too familiar in fact. The parable is not actually about the son, but the father. It is the latter's actions that make the story. The son is commonly understood to have "repented" of his ways and then went home, but that is not exactly what happens. The text does say he "came to his senses," but he does only after he has run through his inheritance, is broke, hungry, and has nowhere else to turn. That has a way of bringing anyone to his or her knees, but it can often be a short lived turn about. The question is what this prodigal did the next day, and the parable doesn't give us an answer, I think intentionally.

The reaction of the older son underscores the potential for future mischief by the prodigal. This brother is filled with righteous anger because the father unconditionally welcomes his younger brother home. His father might want to celebrate, but from where he sat he wanted no part in it. The temptation to attribute jealousy or pettiness to this brother ignores the possibility that his reaction reflects the fact that he knows his younger brother well. Siblings often know more about each other than parents know. So he knows, or at least strongly suspects, that his prodigal brother is coming home because he had no place else to go, and will take off just as quickly once he gets back on his feet.

At the same time, though, the actions and attitude of this older son meant the father had to love him unconditionally just as he loved the prodigal, once again underscoring that the focus of the parable is the father, not the sons. This is the message I believe Jesus intended the parable to convey, that God loves without conditions, and all anyone need do to know it for sure is to come home.

Hebrew scripture says the same thing about God. It speaks of divine compassion, mercy, bountiful goodness, all words that point to love. That love, that compassion, is what prompted God to choose this people and lead them out of Egypt. "I know heard their cry . . . I know their sufferings, and I have come down to deliver them," Torah story declares (Exodus 3:7-8).

The God of Jesus and the God of Israel are one and the same. There is no dual God in scripture, only a God whose love outlasts everything else. Judaism as much as Christianity depends upon and speaks of a God who expects reverence and obedience, but responds to the foolishness of human behavior with redeeming love.

This image of God is very pronounced in the words of the prophet Jeremiah. He more than any of the Hebrew prophets understands God's demand for obedience and faithfulness is exceeded only by the depth of God's love and grace that will not let the people go. On the one hand he speaks stirring words of judgment on the nation, certain that they are doomed to fall under the rule of Babylon. When that in fact happens, however, Jeremiah sees the hope of redemption, of God bringing Israel back home, back to life, back from death. A new Israel will rise up, he says, and will build homes once again in the land of their ancestors (Jeremiah 32:15). More than that God will this time write the law, that is, the conditions of covenant, on the people's hearts rather than leaving it in stone (Jeremiah 31:31-34).

The divine/human drama found in Jeremiah plays out again in the life of Jesus who weeps over a holy city spurning the ways of peace (Luke 19:41-42). The time of judgment has come, yet there are no limits to divine forgiveness (Matthew 18:22).

No other image of God can equal this one. Love truly is the greatest gift, the heart and soul of all relationships, human and divine. From beginning to end scripture declares that love can be trusted to be powerful, persuasive, redemptive, enduring. It will and does outlast everything. It is light shining in darkness. Why? Because it emanates from the very being of God.

Yet people of faith in every generation have struggled with believing in the reality and power of unconditional love. The church has more often than not found itself giving lip service by attaching conditions to God's forgiveness with threatening words to persuade people to dedicate themselves to doing God's will. It is as if the church cannot believe love is enough, that love possesses sufficient power to attract people to goodness. But this is where scripture should shape our faith. It speaks of a faithful God who creates and recreates life because love will not let humanity go. For Christians this message lies at the heart of what it means to follow Jesus. It is why we work for justice in all its manifestations, why we call on nations to choose peace over war, why we believe compassion can change the world. God as love serves as the foundation for everything else we believe about God.

****

Where the image of God as love becomes most critical is in the way Christians understand the meaning of Jesus' death. Through the centuries Christian theologians have sought to understand it as an act of divine justice that satisfied God's anger, paid humanity's debt caused by sin, or in one way or another was a necessary element in God's willingness to forgive and extend grace to all of humankind.

There is, however, another way to think about all of this that makes God's unconditional love the instrument of redemption, reclamation, reconciliation. In other words, the key to God's relationship with creation to which Hebrew and Christian scripture alike testify is love, not fear. It is the way and will of the God of Jesus. It is an image of the divine that invites response rather than demanding it. This is the subject to which we now turn our attention.

CHAPTER FOUR

Jewish Roots of Christian Atonement

ONCE WE UNDERSTAND that all questions lead back to a loving God who is the beginning and end of faith, we are ready to explore the fact that Christians today have much to gain and little to lose in rethinking one of the most basic claims that we make about Jesus: that he died on the cross for our sins. This is what theologians call the doctrine of atonement. The following statement is an excellent summary of what it means.

> *Christians believe God really did atone for sins in Jesus Christ and that God really did redemptively create restored relationships with God, with self, with others, and with the world . . . the atonement, in other words, is the good news of Christianity—it is our gospel. It is how that gospel works.*"⁹

There is, of course, no single view of atonement in the history of Christian thought, but in its fundamental form it says that

God extended forgiveness to humanity through the death of Jesus. In addition, believing in Jesus as savior of the world is a prerequisite for salvation (something I will also discuss later).

While this is what the church says is "the good news of Christianity," it is also the primary theological barrier to Christians who wish to accept the possibility that there are other paths to God. If Jesus died for our sins, to me it seems impossible for Christians to also believe that people from other faiths are saved. We can be respectful of them. We can believe that one day, either in this life or the next, they will acknowledge Jesus as savior and Lord. Or we can just not bring up the subject. But at the end of the day, the logical conclusion of being a Christian necessarily means believing that non-Christians are going to hell.

People attach different meanings to terms such as "salvation," "heaven," and "hell," and we shall see that those differences in understanding are important, but for now it is both sufficient and I think accurate to say that this is the message most churches teach and preach. Salvation depends upon the crucifixion, wherein God extended forgiveness of sin to anyone who accepts Jesus as savior.

This form of atonement theology is called substitutionary and is the most dominant one in the West.[10] Ask any American Christian what the church says is the reason Jesus died on the cross and he or she will likely answer that he died for our sins.[11] This is actually a bit ironic, given the fact that as rigid as the church has been theologically because of its creedal formulations, it was far less so about the meaning of Jesus' death until recent centuries. Today the death of Jesus stands "not only in the center of church life, but at the heart of Western thought and culture."[12]

Atonement is a subject that has been the focus of intense and ongoing debate within the church almost since its beginning. Irenaeus, a second-century Christian apologist, understood Jesus' death as "recapitulative redemption," to use the modern phrase attached to his view. According to this view, Adam disobeyed God and brought sin and death to humanity. Jesus was perfectly obedient to the point of accepting the cross, canceling out the effects of Adam's disobedience.

In the twelfth century, St. Anselm, Archbishop of Canterbury, declared that Jesus' death was a ransom paid to God for the redemption of the world. Jesus was, Anselm said, a substitute given by God on behalf of humankind to satisfy the demands of God's honor. The substitutionary suffering of Jesus on the Cross was, he further declared, an example of divine mercy.

> *For, indeed, what greater mercy could be imagined than for God the Father to say to the sinner, condemned to eternal torments, and without any power of redeeming himself from them, "Receive my only-begotten Son, and give him to yourself," and for the Son himself to say, "Take me, and redeem yourself?" For they as much as say this when they call us and draw us to Christian faith.*

Protestant Reformers such as John Calvin expanded on Anselm's work by insisting that Jesus' death was not necessary to satisfy God's honor, but was the means by which God's wrath or anger was appeased. This came to be known as "penal substitution" atonement, wherein Jesus suffered what God intended humanity to suffer, and in doing so God's anger was quelled and God's justice upheld.

ATONEMENT AND THE NEW TESTAMENT

It is difficult to avoid the fact that Anselm's ransom/ substitutionary atonement theory seems to be rooted in the New Testament itself.

Consider, for example, the words of Jesus: ". . . whoever wishes to be great among you must be your servant, and whoever wishes to be first among you must be your slave; just as the Son of Man came not to be served but to serve, and to give his life a ransom for many" (Matthew 20:26-28).

The Apostle Paul said he proclaimed "Christ crucified,

a stumbling block to Jews and foolishness to Gentiles." In his letter to the Romans he wrote: "For there is no distinction, since all have sinned and fallen short of the glory of God; they are now justified by his grace as a gift, through the redemption that is in Christ Jesus, whom God put forward as a sacrifice of atonement by his blood, effective through faith" (Romans 3:23-25).

The writer of Hebrews declared: "Therefore he had to become like his brothers and sisters in every respect, so that he might be a merciful and faithful high priest in the service of God, to make a sacrifice of atonement for the sins of the people" (2:17).

John's gospel: "The next day [John] saw Jesus coming toward him and declared, "Here is the Lamb of God who takes away the sin of the world!" (John 1:29).

And in 1 John 2:2 we read: ". . . and he is the atoning sacrifice for our sins, and not for ours only but also for the sins of the whole world."

These are among the texts most often cited to prove Jesus died for our sins, leading some scholars to conclude this is the heart of the Christian message. As one put it:

Jesus is Savior of Jews and non-Jews alike, primarily because of the atoning value of his death on the cross. In short, by dying on the cross, Jesus paid for the sins of humanity. This is the teaching of all of Christianity's earliest teachers and writers. Not every New Testament writing speaks to this topic, of course, but most do, and not one suggests an alternative understanding of Jesus' death.[13]

But is this actually the case? Did Jesus think of his impending death as sacrificial? And do these New Testament texts intend for us to understand them as saying Jesus literally took our place on the Cross? If the words "ransom" and "redemption" were intended to be taken literally, then the answer is "yes." A ransom means something is paid in order for something else to happen.

A Different Jesus

Understood in this way, Jesus' death literally "paid" the price or ransom necessary for human beings to be forgiven.

But to whom was this ransom paid? Was Irenaeus right when he said it was paid to Satan? Or were Anselm and Calvin right when they insisted it was paid to God? If to God, then the God who is love must be understood as One viewing humanity as "slaves" whose lives had to be ransomed in order to avoid eternal condemnation. Nothing in the teachings of Jesus suggests this is the God he served or the God whose will he charged his followers to obey. On the contrary, in the words of John's gospel, we are the children of God (John 1:12).

But setting aside the fact that slave language when referencing the divine/human relationship is fraught with difficulties, the real problem lies in the fact that to understand Jesus as a substitutionary sacrifice for human sin assumes that New Testament language was literal, rather than metaphorical as it was used in Hebrew scripture. When "ransom" is used to refer to God bringing the Hebrew slaves out of Egypt, the Torah is speaking metaphorically. No ransom was paid to Pharaoh literally. Because the story is about the children of Abraham being made slaves in Egypt, "ransom" was an image the people knew well. It is not surprising, then, that we read the words, "I am the Lord your God, who brought you out of the land of Egypt, out of the house of slavery" (Exodus 20:2). This is not language to be taken literally, but is the image of God as Israel's deliverer (Isaiah 19:20).

This is why John 1:29 is a rather confusing statement. John presents Jesus as the Passover paschal lamb, yet the paschal lamb is not about sin offerings. It was a symbol of freedom from Egypt, the "ransom" paid for the Hebrew slaves. If we understand words such as "ransom" and "redemption" metaphorically in the same way we can read the Genesis 1 creation story, the theological significance of the meaning of Jesus' death is not that ransom was paid to God. Rather, it is that the death of Jesus was understood by the early church as a saving act similar to God bringing Hebrew slaves out of Egypt.[14]

THE PROBLEMS OF ORIGINAL SIN

Complicating the issue of the meaning of Jesus' death is the concept of Original Sin. Irenaeus first posited the notion of Original Sin, but the concept was brought to full prominence by St. Augustine in the fourth century. In his zeal to refute Pelagianism—the belief that human beings possessed an inherit capacity to do good—Augustine interpreted the words of the Apostle Paul in Romans 5:12-17 to say that Adam's sin was conveyed to all of humanity through sensual desire that corrupted free will. Paul wrote:

> *Therefore, just as sin came into the world through one man, and death came through sin, and so death spread to all because all have sinned . . . Yet death exercised dominion from Adam to Moses, even over those whose sins were not like the transgression of Adam, who is a type of the one who was to come.*
>
> *For if the many died through the one man's trespass, much more surely have the grace of God and the free gift in the grace of the one man, Jesus Christ, abounded for the many. And the free gift is not like the effect of the one man's sin. For the judgment following one trespass brought condemnation, but the free gift following many trespasses brings justification. If, because of the one man's trespass, death exercised dominion through that one, much more surely will those who receive the abundance of grace and the free gift of righteousness exercise dominion in life through the one man, Jesus Christ (Romans 5:12-17).*

On first glance Paul does seem to be saying what Augustine thought, that Adam (and Eve) brought the disease of sin into the world and it infected the whole of humanity; and that Jesus' death was the means by which God graciously erased the consequences of that disease, though it still exists. But even Paul's imagery is anything but clear. He speaks of some "whose sins were not like the transgression of Adam." Who are they? In addition, Jesus' death remedied the sins of those like Adam. How? Or, knowing what we know about the human psyche today, is it sensible to insist that we must accept Paul's belief that sexual desire was a sign of sin? Perhaps more likely is that Augustine's interpretation of the apostle's words was a reflection of an unresolved inner conflict in the great man that was rooted in his own sensual ways before he became a Christian.

That scholars offer different interpretations of what Paul meant, some agreeing with Augustine and some not, is itself a reason for caution when Christians assume that what they mean when using language found in the New Testament is the same as what the writers meant.[15] Moreover, we need to remember that in this passage Paul is making the argument that Jesus was the antidote to the sin of Adam, even though he would have known as surely as any informed Jew of his day that in Hebrew the word used for "Adam" was not a reference to a single man but to "mankind," or humanity as a whole. Thus, it is quite plausible to suggest that Paul is making an analogy between Adam and Christ— humankind and Messiah—to underscore his belief that divine grace is the only source of human "righteousness," or the human capacity to act justly.

At the very least we know that Original Sin does not reflect the core teachings of the Judaism that Jesus, Paul, and all his first followers embraced. "Judaism does not have a teaching of 'original sin' per se," writes Professor Amy-Jill Levine, "it does not presuppose a negative anthropology in which humanity exists in a state of alienation from God. Thus it does not require the sacrifice of the Christ to rectify the original breach."[16]

She goes on to point out that Judaism does not ignore the story of Adam's sin. But God is the One who restores humanity to a right relationship with the Divine without the need of human sacrifice. "The Holy One," she writes, "deprived Adam of six things: splendor of visage, lofty statue, life without death, perfection of the earth's fruit, the Garden of Eden, and the brilliance of the luminaries in heaven. In the time to come, the Holy One will restore them."[17]

In addition to the conflict between Original Sin and Judaism, today's Christian must also grapple with the fact that the concept stands in contradistinction to evolutionary biology. Theologian Ronald Goetz spent his entire career wrestling with what he saw as the failure of mainstream theology in the West to integrate evolutionary theory into its understanding of any redemptive meaning of Jesus' death. He went so far as to say that Western Trinitarian theology treats the death of Jesus as if Charles Darwin never lived, meaning atonement theology has for too long ignored the implications of human evolution on the nature of being human.

Goetz was no apologist for Darwin. He simply wanted Christian theology to come clean and admit that Darwin's work makes the doctrine of Original Sin indefensible. In his own words: "My intention is . . . to show that Darwin's demonstration of the primordially violent nature of biological existence forces a radical, if long delayed, recasting of Trinitarian theology with reference to creation, evil, sin, suffering, and finally, the atoning death of Jesus Christ."[18]

Though this book goes in a very different direction regarding atonement theology than the theology Professor Goetz was writing at the time of his untimely death, it is noteworthy that a theologian of his stature spoke candidly about the need for radical rethinking of this basic teaching of the church.

SACRIFICIAL OFFERINGS

Beyond the problems with the doctrine of Original Sin serving as a foundational piece for substitutionary atonement, traditional Christian understanding of sin offerings does not necessarily accurately represents what the Bible actually says about them.

Some scholars think the Old Testament is ambiguous about the practice of human sacrifice in ancient Israel, especially before the giving of the Law. But in the Torah there are texts that state clearly that God abhors such sacrifice. And in contrast to the practice by other nations, Deuteronomy 12:31 declares: "You must not do the same for the Lord your God, because every abhorrent thing that the Lord hates they have done for their gods. They would even burn their sons and their daughters in the fire to their gods." The Torah also tells the story of Abraham being willing to sacrifice his son, Isaac, but in the end God stops him before he does.

I read the Abraham/Isaac story as Torah material that rejects the practice of child sacrifice, but some rabbinical literature, especially in the Middle Ages, takes a different view.[19] That said, we know that by the first century Judaism had flatly rejected human sacrifice as an acceptable Temple ritual. In the context of the practice of animal sacrifice in ancient Israel, then, when Jesus and his followers talked about his death being a sacrifice for sin, it is likely that they were speaking figuratively, or metaphorically, if you will.

That in fact seems to be how sacrifice was understood in Judaism. Sin offerings were not to be taken literally. No one believed a slain lamb forgave them of their sins, or that God's forgiveness depended on it being done. Nor did the people believe a goat sent into the wilderness actually bore their sins on its head. The Torah says that a sin offering consists of presenting an unblemished goat or lamb to the priest, who will burn it on the temple altar, thus making atonement on behalf of the petitioner whose sin is then forgiven (Leviticus 4:27-35). It was a ritual symbolizing God's forgiveness, which is why in all likelihood Jesus used this language.

Also important to note is the fact that these rituals were not for willful sin, but for the unwitting sin of the people. "If anyone of the ordinary people among you sins unintentionally," Leviticus 4:27 declares. The law existed to exact punishment for intentional violations. Sin offerings were always for those sins done unintentionally and even unconsciously.

That sacrificial rituals were symbolic may be one of the reasons Jewish hopes for a messiah did not include the concept of a suffering messiah who would become a sacrifice for sin. The messiah might suffer, but not in the sense of being a human sacrifice to God. For this reason the Christian use of the suffering servant motif in Isaiah 53 as a messianic passage justifying substitutionary atonement goes beyond what the text actually says. Indeed, because chapter 42:5-7 speaks of Israel as God's servant, many scholars argue that it is the nation rather than an individual who is the suffering servant Isaiah had in mind:

Thus says God, the LORD,
who created the heavens and stretched them out,
who spread out the earth and what comes from it,
who gives breath to the people upon it
and spirit to those who walk in it:
I am the LORD, I have called you in righteousness,
I have taken you by the hand and kept you;
I have given you as a covenant to the people,
a light to the nations,
to open the eyes that are blind,
to bring out the prisoners from the dungeon,
from the prison those who sit in darkness.

But even if this is not the case, the concept of a human sacrifice is not a part of Israel's prophetic tradition. For this reason the focus of the poem found in Isaiah 53:1-12 can be understood as a poignant expression of hope for a restored Israel Isaiah declares will happen through suffering that is redemptive. Thus he writes:

He was despised and rejected by others;
a man of suffering and acquainted with infirmity;
and as one from whom others hide their faces
he was despised, and we held him of no account.
Surely he has borne our infirmities
and carried our diseases;
yet we accounted him stricken,
struck down by God, and afflicted.

But he was wounded for our transgressions,
crushed for our iniquities;
upon him was the punishment that made us whole,
and by his bruises we are healed.

(Isaiah 53:3-5)

For Christians who believe Jesus died for the sins of the world, it is not surprising that Isaiah's words would be understood as a description of why he was crucified. But saying this was the meaning the prophet intended is another matter altogether. Indeed, a suffering messiah was not what the people expected from God. They believed, instead, that God would honor the covenant made with their ancestors, bring the people back from Babylon, and reestablish Israel as a covenant partner.

Certainly no Jewish interpreters today understand this text as foreshadowing the death of Jesus. The most we can say is that they might hear them as a description of what the nation as a whole underwent before their return from Exile around 535 BCE. For Christians who do not embrace atonement theology, Isaiah's words might even speak of the redemptive nature of all innocent suffering that Jesus himself did actually experience. British scholar N. T. Wright goes a step further in suggesting that the suffering servant motif describes the vocational role of Israel for the sake of the world that had been all but lost until Jesus embraced it for himself.[20] I believe that is as far as we can reasonably go in appropriating this prophetic passage into any understanding of Jesus as messiah.

CHAPTER FIVE

Jesus and the Salvation of Christians

UNDERSTANDING NEW TESTAMENT language that interprets the meaning of Jesus' death metaphorically invites us to rethink the way Christian theology has understood salvation itself. Instead of salvation being made possible through a ransom paid to satisfy God's honor or anger because of sin, it can be understood as an act of God that saved all humanity from ultimate isolation from God. But . . . this act of God was not the death of Jesus, but his resurrection.

HISTORICAL REVERSAL

Shifting attention from Jesus' crucifixion to his resurrection is the point to which we are moving, but we are not there yet. First we need to put that shift in historical context. Christian exclusivism or triumphalism that insists Jesus is the only way to salvation actually represents a stunning reversal of history. Given the fact that initially all first-century Christians were Jewish, the primary issue nascent Christianity faced during the time of the Apostle Paul was what to do about non-Jews who were becoming Christian. Jews believed they were under covenant with God through Moses. Gentiles knew nothing of Torah Law. Most of the first Christians believed that they should become Jews as well as Christians. Paul did not, and in the end he won the argument. Within a generation the church was mostly Gentile, the number of Jewish Christians a minority. Looking back, we can see that this development is what led Christians to posit the argument that they alone were "saved" and that all non-Christians had to be converted to be accepted by God.

The picture now comes into focus. Christians questioning the fate of non-Christians was born of the changed makeup of the church's membership. Because most Jews chose not to join the Jesus movement, by the end of the first century more non-Jews were Christians than Jews. Still a sect within Judaism, growth in the number of Gentiles becoming followers of Jesus saw the original tensions between Jews and Jewish Christians morph into tensions between Jews and the Jesus movement. It was not until four centuries later that Christianity became a recognized religion in the Roman Empire distinct from Judaism.

RADICAL MONOTHEISM

Various reasons are cited for why over time most Jews chose to remain Jews and not become Christians, but the most obvious contributing fact is often most overlooked. It was—and is to this day—their radical monotheistic faith in One God. This is why the doctrine of the Holy Trinity or the concept of One God in Three Persons is so troublesome to them.

Though not explicitly stated in New Testament material, the veneration of Jesus in the early history of the church—perhaps even before the end of the first century—forced the church to think of who Jesus was within the limitation of monotheistic restraints. Jesus as divine could not be sustained apart from his being an expression of or somehow "of one substance" with God. The same dynamic was at work with the Holy Spirit, so that Jesus and the Spirit were the same as God because there is only one God. The point was not to make Jesus divine as much as to preserve monotheism within Christian thinking.

Despite efforts to this end, though, Trinitarianism was not able to overcome the demands of monotheism in the minds of Jews. That is why the suggestion that Jesus was God, or equal to God, or the second person of some ineffable God-Head, would have been considered by Jews at the time of Jesus, and to Jesus himself, as an idolatrous claim, not least because it would have undermined the most fundamental belief in Judaism, that there is only one true God.[21]

Radical monotheism formed the core of Israel's faith. The first commandment says no other gods before the God of Israel. Even as a tacit acknowledgement of the existence of other gods, only Yahweh is to be worshipped. There was no God-Head, only God. The spirit ("ruah") of God in Hebrew scripture was not a different member of the God-Head. God's spirit was the way Judaism spoke of God's presence and God's work on Israel's behalf. The idea of a man being God in any form, or equal to God in any way, would have been anathema to Jewish monotheism, something the early Christians who were Jews first apparently understood. "Let the same mind be in you that was in Christ Jesus," they sang, "who, though he was in the form of God, did not regard equality with God as something to be exploited, but emptied himself, taking the form of a slave, being born in human likeness" (a portion of an early hymn found in Philippians 2:5-7).

Likewise, it is simply unthinkable that Jesus, Jew that he was, thought of himself as God. Indeed, he prayed to God. He spoke of being sent by God. In Gethsemane he petitioned for God to let the cup of suffering pass over him. But in claiming Jesus was equal with God—indeed, was God—church creeds leave us with no choice but to believe he was praying to himself, having sent himself to earth, and at the end of his earthly life was begging to be released from suffering himself.

Not intending to be sarcastic, my point is this. The first question that the claim that Jesus was God or equal to God must answer is how Jesus could have ever believed such a thing given the radical monotheism of Judaism itself. Moreover, this question suggests that texts often cited to prove Jesus was God may not have that meaning at all. When Jesus prays for his disciples in John 17, for example, and refers to his "oneness" with God (". . . so that they may be one, as we are one" [eis]—John 17:23), he is not saying that he and God are the "same." The meaning of the word is "one," not "same." Thus Jesus is asking God (not himself) to bring his disciples into a relationship with one another that parallels the "oneness" he has experienced with God, so that the world will know they belong to him.

Another example is Jesus being described by the writer of John's gospel as the "word" made flesh. The actual text reads: "And the Word became flesh and encamped with us" (John 1:14). In Hebrew tradition Moses pitched a tent, which became the "tent of meeting" between God and Moses and God and the people. That may well have been the intention of John's description of Jesus as God's "pitched tent," an image that first-century Jews would have immediately understood.

In the ancient world there was a common belief that "words" had power because the essence of a person was contained in them. When God spoke creation into existence ("And God said . . ."), the Genesis writer was suggesting that creation held something of the essence of the Creator in it. This may also have been what John was saying about Jesus. He was God "speaking" once again, and as such, was something of the essence of God in the world. This is a meaning first-century Jews would have understood without believing it meant that Jesus was God. The prophets had spoken the word of God before Jesus, also embodying the essence of God to Israel.

Given, then, the historical context of Jesus' life, and the

Jewishness of the first Christians who formed the Jesus movement, the belief that Jesus was divine in the sense that he was God, equal to God, or of the same substance as God, must be seen as the church's misunderstanding of what the phrase "Son of God" would have meant to Jesus and those who believed he was the Messiah.

This mistake does not have to be ours. The Jesus that Christians today follow is worthy of our trust, not because he was divine, but precisely because he was as human as we are, gave his life fully to God, was killed for his devotion, and was raised to new life by the God he trusted. Thus, salvation is not about his death making God's forgiveness possible. It has, instead, everything to do with God declaring in Jesus' resurrection that "neither death, nor life, nor angels, nor rulers, nor things present, nor things to come, nor powers, nor height, nor depth, nor anything else in all creation, will be able to separate us from the love of God in Christ Jesus our Lord" (Romans 8:38-39).

The gospel of Jesus Christ, then, is not about his crucifixion. It is about his resurrection, an event that includes all and excludes none. That now becomes our focus.

CHAPTER SIX

Resurrection Salvation

WE NOW COME to the heart of the matter, the bodily resurrection of Jesus.[22]

As long as the crucifixion remains the anchor for the Christian message, the resurrection necessarily stands in its shadow. That is unfortunate since the resurrection is the cornerstone of Christianity and the reason the Christian community emerged to tell Jesus' story. In other words, *the Christian community was not born at the foot of the cross, but at the door of an empty tomb.*

The resurrection is the message the New Testament writers wanted to proclaim. But as is the case with most beliefs, there is no consensus among Christians today about what actually happened in the event we call the resurrection of Jesus. The position I want to argue for here is the bodily resurrection of Jesus, which is probably a minority position to take among scholars and clergy. But it is the perspective I believe that makes the most sense in accounting for the radical change in the disciples before and after Jesus' crucifixion.[23] What's more, it is the message I think the gospel writers intended to convey.

THE GOSPELS AND THE RESURRECTION

While each of the four gospels describes the resurrection in different ways, all unequivocally declare that it happened. Mark, the shortest and most cryptic of them, explicitly says the "young man" the three women saw when they entered the tomb said Jesus was raised: But he said to them, "Do not be alarmed; you are looking for Jesus of Nazareth, who was crucified. He has been raised; he is not here. Look, there is the place they laid him" (Mark 16:6). He then tells them to inform the disciples that this has happened, and also to tell them Jesus will meet them in Galilee. For reasons Mark does not give, the women were so confounded by what they had witnessed that they didn't tell anyone (16:8).

What is curious about many interpretations of this text is that they insist that because it says the women said nothing to anyone, this oldest of the gospels cannot be included with the others in saying there was a resurrection, especially since the appearance stories in the last half of Mark 16 are not in the earliest versions of the gospel. The problem, though, is that whatever Mark may have intended to say by telling us the women said nothing, it makes no sense to think it was a subtle way to undercut the "young man's" message that Jesus had been raised. To ignore what the text actually says is an example of skepticism looking for a justification.

The other three gospels provide further resurrection confirmation of what Mark does in fact say. In Matthew's account, two women—Mary Magdalene and another Mary (perhaps the mother of Jesus)—are told by an angel (not unlike the "young man") that Jesus has been raised (28:6). They were also instructed to tell the disciples that Jesus would meet them in Galilee, just as Mark's gospel says. Then Matthew adds that Jesus met the women before they could leave and confirmed the angel's instructions (9-10), followed by the story of the Temple leaders' plan to say Jesus' body had been stolen (11-15).

Luke's gospel contains the story of two men meeting Jesus on the road to Emmaus (24:13-35). He says that when the two went back to Jerusalem and told the others of their experience, Jesus appeared to them all, invited them to touch his wounds, sat and ate with them, and then reminded them of scripture they should have known that predicted his being raised (24:44-49). What then follows is Luke's version of Jesus' ascension (50-53), which is also recorded in Acts 1:9-11.

John's gospel includes more stories of Jesus' post-resurrection appearances than any of the others. First Jesus meets Mary Magdalene at the tomb (20:11-18), similar to the other three gospels, followed by an appearance before all the disciples (19-23) and the encounter with Thomas, who is the one who must be convinced Jesus is alive (24-29). John then breaks into these post-resurrection stories to tell us Jesus said and did many other things not reported in his gospel, followed by an explanation for why he told the ones he did ("that through believing you may have life in his name"—20:30-31). John then describes another resurrection experience, this one about Jesus appearing before seven other disciples by the sea of Tiberias (21:1-3), followed by the story of Peter jumping out of the boat and running to meet Jesus (21:4-8). Afterward Jesus eats with the disciples (9-14), John adding that this was the third time Jesus had appeared to the disciples. After they had finished the meal, Jesus asked Peter three times if he loves him (15-19). Finally, Jesus encounters the beloved disciple John, whom the gospel uses to correct an apparent rumor going around that Jesus had said that this special disciple would never die (v.23). The gospel ends with a statement that this same disciple was the source of John's material (24-25).

FACT OR FICTION?

It is, of course, always possible that Matthew, Luke, and John made up their stories about the raised Jesus and his appearing to the disciples, but nothing in the stories themselves rules out the possibility that they didn't. Language that speaks of angels and special messengers is common in scripture; such imagery was not out of step with the way the world was understood at the time. But the reality of the event they are describing does not depend upon such imagery. If I said God called me into ministry, you might find such language out of character with the way you see the world. You might even wonder if I thought I actually heard God speaking audibly. But what you cannot say is that my way of describing the moment I decided to enter into ministry proves that my experience of being "called" by God into ministry was imagined, not real.

Biblical images, metaphors, and language reflect the world of those who wrote the Bible, but the events they describe may have actually happened nonetheless. I don't believe in angels myself, but I do believe the gospel writers were using such language to convey a message that was true. The Jesus they saw crucified was alive.

Another example of why the gospel accounts of Jesus being raised from the dead can be considered reliable is the fact that Matthew includes the story of the plot to steal Jesus' body. Put simply, he may have done so because this is precisely the story the Temple priests told to undercut the claims that Jesus was alive. It is actually quite plausible that they would concoct such a story as a way to put a quick end to having to deal with Jesus and his followers again after they had just colluded with Roman authorities to put Jesus to death. It is a logical explanation for the body's disappearance, except that we have nothing to indicate it was ever found or the theft was finally confirmed.

Luke's story of the Emmaus encounter of the two disciples with Jesus also rings true. He may have created it, of course, but it is also possible that he found it to be an example of why a later generation of Christians might also believe that they, too, could experience the living presence of Jesus—just as the two on the road did unexpectedly—in the breaking of bread, something, by the way, the church today says is still possible.

We can also say that John's gospel, coming as it did toward the end of the first century, might have included resurrection stories that were complete fabrications as an attempt to shore up a dying Christian community, and perhaps even a dying Christianity. Or he may have told all the stories he did because his gospel was written late enough to have allowed the many and various stories about the resurrection to become widely known in Christian circles. The historical reliability of this possibility is strengthened by the fact that the late date of the gospel meant ample time had passed for the resurrection appearance stories to have been exposed as false, yet that had not happened. Almost seventy years had passed since the event, and the stories about it were still gaining in their power to attract belief.

It is true that resurrection stories were not unknown in the Greco-Roman world (and also in Buddhism and Hinduism), but only those about Jesus rose above the level of mythology and become the foundational claim of a sustainable community of faith.

I also believe the symmetry in John's story of Jesus asking Peter three times for complete devotion (21:15-19) with such a well-known story of Peter's three denials of Jesus (18:15-27), which appears in all four gospels, increases its historical reliability. Surely John would have known that fabricating a story to parallel one of the most well-known events in the life of one of the major early Christian leaders would have invited scrutiny, if not outright skepticism, unless it was widely known to have been told by Peter and the others present.

MORE THAN THE GOSPELS

While arguments against the historical reliability of the gospel accounts of Jesus' resurrection should not be dismissed entirely, I have tried to show that the very reasons skeptics offer for rejecting them can serve as reasons to believe them. Moreover, it is unequivocally clear that the gospel writers were not using cryptic imagery to describe something that happened to the disciples inwardly. That is to say, the gospels do not use metaphors to say that it was Jesus' teachings that were resurrected after his death, or that the disciples' memories of Jesus made them *feel* like he was still alive. Believe them or not, the gospels say Jesus of Nazareth was raised from the dead.

But in fact we have much more than the gospels to support the bodily resurrection of Jesus,[24] none more emphatic than what the Apostle Paul said about it:

> *Now if Christ is proclaimed as raised from the dead, how can some of you say there is no resurrection of the dead? If there is no resurrection of the dead, then Christ has not been raised; and if Christ has not been raised, then our proclamation has been in vain and your faith has been in vain. We are even found to be misrepresenting God, because we testified of God that he raised Christ—whom he did not raise if it is true that the dead are not raised. For if the dead are not raised, then Christ has not been raised. If Christ has not been raised, your faith is futile and you are still in your sins (1 Corinthians 15:12-17).*

Paul also says Jesus appeared to more than five hundred people (1 Corinthians 15:6), one of whom was himself. His Damascus Road encounter (Acts 9:1-9) was the foundation for Paul's focus on Jesus' resurrection, as well as his becoming an apostle for the Christian message in its entirety. Whatever else that can be said about the resurrection of Jesus, history has shown that Paul's quick recognition that it was the heart and soul of Christian belief proved to be true.

It is also what produced the Jesus movement that became the church. Within weeks the disciples who, according to the gospel accounts, had all abandoned Jesus (Mark 14:50) were emboldened to publicly declare that Jesus had been raised. That change is the reason the church exists today. It is possible that hallucinatory visions are what led them to say this, but it is equally possible that they did because what they experienced was real, not least because God is.[25]

IT'S ABOUT GOD

When you think about it, the message that Jesus had been raised from the dead was a bold and provocative claim whose falsehood could have easily been exposed. Yet it wasn't, and never has been, leaving us to respond either yea or nay to the New Testament message that *God* raised the crucified Jesus to life again.

Of course, believing Jesus was raised from the dead is a statement of faith, which, as noted in chapter 1 regarding all such claims, doesn't make it true. What's more, we live in a world where science is unmasking more and more secrets of the universe and the building blocks of life itself. Faith cannot deny that we now know more about the human body and the laws of nature than the ancients could have possibly known. This matters, which is why making a case for the resurrection faces stiff odds. It should come as no surprise that believing Jesus was actually raised from the dead is a minority view among scholars, probably most mainline pastors, and perhaps more than a few church members. That the disciples experienced something powerful after the crucifixion that led them to say Jesus was alive is evident enough, but that it was actually a bodily resurrection is not. So while we have personal testimony in the New Testament to the resurrection of Jesus, whether or not today's Christians have any real basis for accepting it remains an open question.

But perhaps not for long, at least for people of faith. I say that because the first thing all Christians should understand is that the resurrection is not really about Jesus. It is about God; specifically, that God actually exists. This is why I began this book with God. Believing God is real is the context for understanding something like the resurrection. God is where everything begins, just as the

Genesis writer said: "In the beginning God created the heavens and the earth" (1:1). Both Genesis creation stories arise from an already accepted belief that God exists. To say God is the source of creation and the author of life presupposes that God is.

This is also the theological foundation for the resurrection of Jesus. Just as the Genesis writers sought to understand creation within the context of their choice to believe in God, the resurrection needs to be understood in the same context. If you believe in God, you have chosen to agree with the Genesis writer that in whatever way life on this planet emerged, God was there at the beginning.

Claiming Jesus was raised to new life is a similar kind of affirmation. It depends upon and is an extension of the belief that God was and is the Creator of life. In other words, to believe in the resurrection is to believe the One who created life in the first place is the One who brought Jesus back from the dead. Jesus didn't raise himself. He didn't just wake up after three days and roll away the stone at the grave. The gospels say the resurrection happened because God acted to bring Jesus back to life. The people who knew him before his death met him again afterward and testified that he was alive.[26]

The resurrection stories in the New Testament are intended to convey the message that Jesus, the person the disciples had followed, was alive in the flesh. His body was real, yet it became apparent that it was also different. He was with them and then he was gone, appearing and disappearing from their midst. There was no later death because he had not been resuscitated, but instead raised with what the Apostle Paul called a "spiritual body" (1 Corinthians 15:44). And it was this body that made him known to the disciples and at the same time was not "physical" in the same way as before his death. What mattered was that they became convinced he was alive. The leap for them was not as great as it may appear to us, because they already believed God was real and that all things were possible with and because of God.

The gospel accounts of the resurrection of Jesus, then, tell of life born and reborn. The God of creation who authored life is the One who raised Jesus from the dead.

MIRACLES AND FAITH

Since believing in the resurrection of Jesus means believing in an extraordinary occurrence in history, it is natural to place it in the category of "miracle." It fits the definition, which is "an unusual or wonderful event that is believed to be caused by the power of God." We can see why people who don't believe in God don't believe in miracles. The prerequisite for entertaining the possibility of miracles is the choice to believe in God.

That choice means many things, but the fundamental and foundational one is accepting the fact that if God is God, it follows that God must be free to do what God chooses to do. In other words, believing in God includes believing in the absolute freedom of God's sovereignty. That is why miracles happened unexpectedly. A God who is real must ultimately be sovereign and free. If this were not the case, God would then be subject to limitations placed on God. For all practical purposes this would mean people created God rather than the other way around.

A miracle, then, is a moment when God acts because God is free to act. Does this raise the question about why a good God does not always act to avert suffering and pain in the world? Of course it does, which is why it is the fundamental challenge atheists make to the existence of a good God. But that question simply raises others equally unanswerable. At the least, it seems to me people of faith and no faith can agree that there is no answer to why one miracle happens and another doesn't. A colleague offered an insightful comment after reading this statement. He wrote:

> *But it may have something to do with how God respects the integrity of creation and how one miracle may not lead to a destructive chain of cause and effect and another possible miracle*

would. To control the whole chain of cause and effect would demand reshaping the entire world.[27]

His concern, one I also share, is that God be understood as the Creator who knows the effects of every cause and, thus, does not act capriciously. That said, we nonetheless face the reality that believing in God does not mean we understand all the ways of God. We can affirm that God is always free to act without also having to explain why God doesn't act in ways we suppose God should. Faith in God points only to possibilities, not necessities. Thus, calling an unusual or wonderful event a miracle doesn't require you to explain why another unusual or wonderful event you wanted to happen or believed should have happened didn't. To believe in miracles is simply another way to say you believe in God.

It is also the case that miracles are events we name as such. Something good and wonderful happens and we say it was because of the hand of God. It is possible that there is another explanation for an event happening, such as a man having superhuman strength in lifting a car off a child. Today we know the physiological reasons that can happen. But the resurrection is a different event altogether, an event where another explanation is not plausible. Human beings are not capable of raising someone from the dead. So for anyone who believes in God, it makes sense to call what happened a miracle, because from the perspective of faith that is the only logical explanation for it. The alternative is that it didn't happen at all, but, as I have said, that goes against eyewitness accounts to the contrary. Thus, it is just as reasonable to believe it happened as not to believe it.

RESURRECTION SALVATION

What I am saying, then, is that accepting divine sovereignty as endemic to believing in God means a miracle is always possible, but not always predictable, and that divine limitations are self-imposed. But we can go one step further and say that anything that fits the definition of a miracle must also be consistent with what we believe about the way God relates to humanity and respects the integrity of natural law. Herein is the basis for rejecting substitutionary atonement. Requiring the death of someone in order to forgive others is not consistent with believing in a God who is love.

On the other hand, raising a man who was put to death unjustly is. The resurrection was and is a divine declaration that ultimately the God of creation will redeem and save the whole of creation from the ultimate enemy of life—death. In short, the resurrection of Jesus means divine love wins. The Apostle Paul said as much when he wrote: "O death, where is your sting? O death, where is your victory?" (1 Corinthians 15:55). According to Paul, the heart of Christianity was—and is—that God raised Jesus from the dead, and in doing so declared that nothing in life or death will finally separate us from God (Romans 8:31-39). Moreover, this was an act whose effect necessarily includes the whole of humanity. Jesus being raised was God's declaration that death does not have the final word for anyone. Anyone! Life does. The impact of this gift is universal. From the perspective of scripture, all share in the gift of life God gave at the beginning of history, gave again at the time of Noah, and gave again through Jesus. Just as believing in God leads to the affirmation that we are all one human family, so we are all heirs of the divine promise that nothing will ever separate us from God, including death. This is the resurrection's universal promise of salvation, of being united to God eternally.

From this perspective, Christianity's uniqueness is the universality of the resurrection's promise of oneness with God without end. God could have raised someone else, but our faith is that it was in Jesus' resurrection that God chose to make this message known, and in doing so fulfilled the promise to Abraham that all the world would be blessed through his seed (Geneses 12:3). The resurrection is the basis for saying that the Judeo-Christian heritage was intended to be inclusive rather than exclusive.

UNIVERSAL PARTICULARITY

Once understood for the universal event it was, the resurrection provides Christians with a theological foundation for interfaith relations. As the centerpiece of Christian atonement, the cross of Jesus is inherently exclusive. The resurrection frees us from that kind of triumphalism, which dismisses all other faith traditions out of hand. Instead, the universal nature of Jesus' resurrection allows Christians to be open to examining other faith claims for consistency with their own.

What I am saying also suggests that churches can play a pivotal role in interfaith relations, with renewed focus on the resurrection as the foundation for our life together. In the world we live in, it's inevitable that conflict will follow religion traditions that insist their way is the only way. It may be difficult for us to admit it, but atonement theology as the explanation for why Jesus died on the cross has held Christians captive to an exclusivism that only the resurrection can overcome. The cross is not why Christianity exists. The resurrection is. The cross matters because evil seemed triumphant enough to put Jesus to death for doing nothing more than challenging the status quo of political and religious power of his day. His resurrection was and is the assurance that all earthly power is in the end accountable to God. God has the final word.

The resurrection is the reason Christians need not believe that the validity of our faith depends upon the invalidity of all other religious traditions. The faith of Morris Shapiro and Khaled Elabdi assure me there is more than one path to God, but in no way undermines the one I walk as a Christian. People of faith can rejoice that all of us in our own particular ways are living witnesses to the truth that we are one in the spirit because we are one in God, now and forever.

Here is where my own denominational heritage (the Christian Church, Disciples of Christ) has been a great blessing. From the beginning we have been a community of faith committed to the unity of all Christians. Thus, one of our cornerstone statements of faith is: *We are Christians only, but not the only Christians.* As core to our identity as this statement has been, I now understand that it is too small. We need a theology that allows us to say with equal openness: *We are the people of God only, but not the only people of God.* Focusing on Jesus' resurrection rather than his crucifixion is the theological path to that end.

CHAPTER SEVEN

Jesus and the Kingdom of God

A PIVOTAL BY-PRODUCT OF focusing on the here and now is that it directs our attention to the essence of the real message of Jesus. With the assurance that our lives have eternal significance through the resurrection of Jesus, we are free to focus on the message he preached and gave to us to teach. That message was from beginning to end about the kingdom of God.

From that time Jesus began to proclaim, "Repent, for the kingdom of heaven has come near" (Matthew 4:17).

To the disciples he said, "As you go, proclaim the good news, 'The kingdom of heaven has come near'" (Matthew 10:7).

But if it is by the Spirit of God that I cast out demons, then the kingdom of God has come to you (Matthew 12:28).

Now after John was arrested, Jesus came to Galilee,

proclaiming the good news of God, and saying, "The time is fulfilled, and the kingdom of God has come near; repent, and believe in the good news" (Mark 1:14-15).

Once Jesus was asked by the Pharisees when the kingdom of God was coming, and he answered, "The kingdom of God is not coming with things that can be observed; nor will they say, 'Look, here it is!' or 'There it is!' For, in fact, the kingdom of God is among you" (Luke 17:20-21).

These are but a few of the direct and indirect references Jesus made to the reality of the kingdom of God making itself known in his ministry. Jesus believed the dawn of the kingdom of God was at hand. Heaven and earth were becoming as one. The will of God in heaven was becoming the will of God on earth, for which Jesus instructed his disciples to pray (Matthew 6:10). The fulfillment of a coming new covenant, as we have noted, was now taking place: "But this is the covenant that I will make with the house of Israel after those days, says the LORD: I will put my law within them, and I will write it on their hearts" (Jeremiah 31:33). This promise is what we as Christians believe was fulfilled in Jesus.

But the people of Jesus' day didn't see it right away. In fact, most of them didn't understand what he was saying. God's kingdom was within rather than without, he said, spiritual, not political, an upside down kingdom where the first is last, servants are leaders, and the poor are filled with good things while the rich are sent away empty. That was not what they were expecting or wanted to hear. They didn't want a call to life, but a call to arms. They wanted an army to be the sign that the day of the Lord had finally come, but Jesus spoke of different signs of the kingdom of God, of the blind seeing, the lame walking, lepers being cleansed, the ears of the deaf opened, and the poor not being forgotten (Matthew 11:2-6). Toward the end of his ministry, when it was apparent the people were not ready to hear the message he was bringing, he sat down on the hillside outside Jerusalem and wept over their missing this time of God's visitation (Luke 19:41-44).

The kingdom of God written on the people's heart as Jesus talked about it must have sounded even more radical when he extended the reign of God to non-Jews as well as Jews, as he did in his sermon in the synagogue in Nazareth (Luke 4:16-30). He reminded them of the time when famine was widespread in Israel and God sent the prophet Elijah to aid a non-Israelite woman and her son in Zarephath of Sidon. He further recalled the time when there were lepers in Israel and God sent the prophet Elisha to heal Naaman the Syrian who was the leader of the Syrian army, Israel's sworn enemy. In both examples Jesus was underscoring the fact that God belongs to no one, including Israel, and was free to be gracious to any and all people.

The Apostle Paul is the one who first understood the implications of this message of God's sovereignty, albeit he came to it through the backdoor. He had preached the message of Jesus in synagogues to little avail. But when he preached to Gentiles they responded. They wanted to follow this Jesus he spoke about, and did in large numbers. Their response convinced him that it was God's intention all along to fulfill the promise to Abraham that through his seed all the earth would be blessed.

This is the message we can take from these events. Jesus was the instrument of God on earth speaking the language of God as Creator of all, not limited to Israel or the Jerusalem temple or the written law. Paul put this message into practice, ensuring that for future generations God would be understood as the Creator of all - Jew or Gentile, male or female, slave or free (Galatians 3:28). This, I believe, is the message we are to teach to the nations (Matthew 28:18-20).

JESUS THE JEW

The kingdom of God is at hand. This is not a warning to get right with God or face the consequences when you die. It is good news that life triumphs over death, good over evil, hope over despair. It is an invitation to believe God is real and open yourself to the experience of the reality you already believe exists. Everything Jesus said has proven itself to be true in real life—that it is more blessed to give than receive, that losing yourself for the sake of others is how you find yourself, that loving your neighbor as you love yourself works for both of you, that life does not consist in the abundance of things, that peace and justice make the world a better place while war and injustice do not. This is the kingdom of God on earth.

The practical impact of becoming a co-creator in the work of God's reign on earth is to become engaged in acts of mercy and love. Jesus left no doubt that this is what he wanted his followers to do.

> *Not everyone who says to me, "Lord, Lord," will enter the kingdom of heaven, but only the one who does the will of my Father in heaven (Matthew 7:21).*
>
> *When the Son of Man comes in his glory, and all the angels with him, then he will sit on the throne of his glory. All the nations will be gathered before him, and he will separate people one from another as a shepherd separates the sheep from the goats, and he will put the sheep at his right hand and the goats at the left. Then the king will say to those at his right hand, "Come, you that are blessed by my Father, inherit the kingdom prepared for you from the foundation of the world; for I was hungry and you gave me food . . ." (Matthew 25:31ff).*
>
> *If any want to become my followers, let them deny themselves and take up their cross and follow me (Mark 8:34).*

In all my years of ministry I have never once been asked by those concerned about my salvation if I fed the hungry, clothed the naked, cared for the sick, or visited the imprisoned. Rather, their sole concern has been what I believed, specifically, did I believe Jesus died for my sins and had I accepted him as my personal savior. But Jesus apparently thought talk was cheap. He said that what he wanted from his followers was a way of life. On top of that, he didn't confine himself to those who followed him. He said "anyone" who does the will of my father enters the kingdom of heaven.

As a Christian looking in, it appears to me as if what Jesus did and said was grounded in the Judaism in which he lived, moved, and had his being. But trying to understand Jesus in his Jewish context has not been paramount in church teaching. Herein lies a great challenge. As Christians we can work at reading the New Testament gospels from the perspective of Jesus being the Jew he actually was, within the limitations that are endemic to the fact that we are not Jews ourselves.[28] But this can open the way for a deeper appreciation for the critical distinction between the faith of Jesus and the church's faith in Jesus.

JESUS THE MESSIAH?

Several things we have been saying are underscored when we see Jesus as a first-century Jew, not least that he was a real human being, of flesh and blood, subject to physical death as all other human beings are. Moreover, it is the Jesus of New Testament gospels who, because he was Jewish, was seen by Roman and Jewish leaders of the day as a man who was undermining religious and political stability. To what extent each played a role in his death and why is a matter of debate, but that he was put to death around the year 33 CE is not. When the church began to force belief in the Jesus of its creeds with the power of the Roman Empire behind it, theology became a tool of propaganda rather than inquiry into truth, and the Jewish Jesus was virtually lost to the Christian community.

The impact of this development was the pedestalization of Jesus as the divine son of God, as if he had not been Jewish at all. A negative impact of pedestalizing Jesus has been to separate him from the core beliefs of first-century Judaism, none more important (as noted earlier) than Torah Decalogue's prohibition of no other gods before the God of Israel. Only Yahweh is to be worshipped, something that has no small impact on the way we understand the meaning of Jesus as Messiah. In the context of Jewish monotheism, there is no substantive basis for believing either Jesus or his disciples would have expected the Messiah to be anything other than a human being.

Again, looking from the outside in, there seems to be little reason to think first-century Jewish expectations of the Messiah would have prepared the first Christians to believe Jesus as Messiah was a divine figure. While it is unclear exactly when Christians began to believe Jesus was divine (whatever they may have meant by that term), it seems very likely that such a belief would have arisen because of non-Jewish influence on the church.[29] Ironically it is the humanity of Jesus that gives credence to the belief that he was the Messiah of Israel who was the herald of God's kingdom on earth. His message was radical to both Jewish and Roman authorities, both of which had vested interests in the status quo, albeit for different reasons. They succeeded in silencing his voice, only to have God raise him from the dead to show that God is not limited by human action or authority.

This is the Jesus of history and the Christ of my faith, the servant of God whose ways reveal the ways of God to me as one of his followers. If someone knows God in another way, that does not diminish my knowing God in and through Jesus. He is the way, the truth, and the life for me. This positive does not need to be validated by a negative. It stands on its own truth.

JESUS, SON OF GOD

When Jesus is understood within first-century Judaism, church creeds describing him as "of the same substance" as God, in short, making him God, seem disconnected from biblical history. The word "son" used in the New Testament to refer to Jesus ("huios") implies a figurative kinship, not a literal one, consistent with the concept in

Hebrew scripture that Israel's king was the "son" of God. It did not mean the people believed kings were God on earth. Rather, they understood the reference to mean that the king was a "representative" of God, one who was to serve in God's place, doing God's will, not his own, because God was the true king of Israel. It is quite likely that this is what those who followed Jesus believed about him. He was God's representative, an instrument of God, without associating the title "son" with his being divine. As N. T. Wright, whose own faith is strongly Trinitarian, cautions: "We must stress that in the first century the regular Jewish meaning of this title [son of God] had nothing to do with an incipient trinitarianism."[30]

The Apostle Paul adds another dimension to Jesus being the Son of God when he begins his Romans letter with the remarkable statement that Jesus was "declared" the Son of God by the resurrection. The word "declared" means "horizon," or "to mark out or to be bound." It also means to be determined or ordained. Paul seems to be saying that Jesus was the Son of God because God declared him to be only after he had been raised from the dead. We find a similar theme in the story of Peter and Cornelius. Once Peter arrived in Caesarea and was welcomed into Cornelius's home, following the vision or dream he had of God instructing him to do so, the text reads:

> *Then Peter began to speak to them: "I truly understand that God shows no partiality, but in every nation anyone who fears him and does what is right is acceptable to him. You know the message he sent to the people of Israel, preaching peace by Jesus Christ—he is Lord of all. That message spread throughout Judea, beginning in Galilee after the baptism that John announced: how God anointed Jesus of Nazareth with the Holy Spirit and with power; how he went about doing good and healing all who were oppressed by the devil, for God was with him. We are witnesses to all that he did both in Judea and in Jerusalem" (Acts 10:34-39).*

Focus on the words: "how God anointed Jesus of Nazareth with the Holy Spirit and with power" (v. 38). The use of the word "anointed" might be a reference to the anointing of Israel's kings, only in this instance it is God doing so to Jesus. From this perspective God is the One who is acting, anointing, declaring, and identifying Jesus as the instrument of God we believe he was.

A FORGIVING GOD

Part of understanding Jesus within his Jewish context is remembering that a fundamental theme in the Old Testament is that God is gracious and forgiving. That is the reason the people made sin offerings. Numerous texts underscore the theme.

Let your steadfast love, O LORD, be upon us, even as we hope in you (Psalm 33:32).

Out of the depths I cry to you, O LORD.
Lord, hear my voice! Let your ears be
Attentive to the voice of my supplications!
If you, O LORD, should mark iniquities,
Lord, who could stand? But there is
forgiveness with you, so that you may be
revered. I wait for the LORD, my soul waits,
and in his word I hope; my soul waits for the Lord.
(Psalm 130:1-6)

Or Psalm 32:1-5, which is an ode to forgiveness:

Happy are those whose transgression is forgiven,
whose sin is covered.
Happy are those to whom the LORD imputes no iniquity,
and in whose spirit there is no deceit.

A Different Jesus

While I kept silence, my body wasted
away through my groaning all day long.
For day and night your hand was heavy upon me;
my strength was dried up as by the heat of summer.

Then I acknowledged my sin to you,
and I did not hide my iniquity;
I said, "I will confess my transgressions to the LORD,"
and you forgave the guilt of my sin.

Israel's confidence in the forgiveness of God rested on the same conviction Christians hold, that God is loving and gracious. If we say, then, that at the time of Jesus the people needed forgiveness, we are affirming that history repeats itself. Time and again Israel stood in need of forgiveness, and received it, even as we do today. Jesus didn't make forgiveness possible. He made it known, afresh. He *revealed* God's forgiveness.

JESUS AS A WAY

I realize that saying Jesus is "a" way contradicts the meaning of the text usually cited to prove he is the *only* way to God. John 14:6 reads: "I am the way, the truth, and the life, no one comes to the Father except by me." Accepting at face value that Jesus actually spoke these words (an issue very much unsettled among scholars), the text can be viewed as neither affirming nor denying that Jesus was the long-awaited Messiah. Nothing in the Old Testament suggests the role of the Messiah included putting Jews back in relationship with God. Rather, the Messiah was to reestablish the kingdom of Israel, which presupposes the covenantal relationship that existed between God and the people.

In this context there would have been no controversy about Jews being in covenant with God. Thus, so firmly was this consciousness among Jews that it hardly seems credible that John's gospel would call it into question in the way Christian belief today seems to do. By interpreting the words of Jesus to imply that he was saying he was the only way to God leaves us no choice but to conclude that he and John both believed the covenant of Moses had been abrogated. That is a serious and rather long leap indeed.

There is another way to understand these words. Putting them in historical context, they can be understood as speaking to a different issue. In the first century, the appearance of someone claiming to be a messiah was not a strange event. So when Jesus' followers made a claim on his behalf, or when he made it for himself, credibility would have been the primary concern. Moreover, given that Jesus, unlike would-be messiahs before him, did not speak about traditional expectations of the Messiah, such as overthrowing foreign domination and reestablishing the kingdom of Israel, the immediate question about who he really was would have arisen. Was he the one for whom they were waiting?

In this historical context, it makes sense to interpret this text as Jesus answering these questions with an implied assurance that he was Israel's Messiah. Further, at the time John wrote his gospel, similar questions about who Jesus was were circulating in the church. People had been told that the end of time was near, but that event had not happened. By the end of the first century, there were Christians who were wondering if they had made a mistake. Was Jesus just another would-be messiah or the real thing? These questions about Jesus may have been why John recorded these words, which are not found in any other gospel. He was reassuring his readers that they could trust what they believed, that Jesus was the way, truth, and life that God had opened to them.

But the deeper question is: "What did Jesus' followers understand his being the way, the truth, and the life to mean?" If not reestablishing the kingdom of Israel, what? We cannot know for sure, but if they looked at Jesus' life and remembered his words, they could have quickly concluded that his way was compassion, his truth was that love was more powerful than hate, and his life was the example of undivided devotion to God. From this perspective it seems inclusive rather than exclusive to believe compassion, love, and putting God first are the way, indeed, the only way, God wants all people to follow.

I believe this way of reading John 14:6 embodies who Jesus was. That the Jesus of the gospels would want his way, truth, and life to be viewed as exclusive strikes me as too inconsistent with what we know about him to be how he would want to be remembered or followed. At the very least this reading of John 14:6 provides a foundation for being Christian without insisting all who are not Christian stand outside the love and grace of God. To underscore this point, I want to share a parable that Jewish scholar Amy-Jill Levine tells.

She imagines herself standing in front of St. Peter at the pearly gates. She immediately begins to ask him if he could speak Greek, where he went when he wandered off in the middle of the book of Acts, how he and Paul resolved their conflict over kosher laws, and others. Peter tells her he is very busy and they can talk later, and she moves on. She then hears a man behind her telling Peter he recognizes the woman (Professor Levine) and knows she is not a Christian. Pointing to John 14:6 in his red letter edition of the Bible, where Jesus says he is the way, the man insists, "She shouldn't be here."

Peter sighs and leaves the scene only to return with Jesus, who asks the man what the problem is. The man responds, "I don't mean to be rude, but didn't you say that no one comes to the Father except through you?"

Jesus acknowledges that the gospel of John does have him saying those words, but then points out that Matthew has him saying that at the judgment everyone will be evaluated based on how well they lived a righteous life, including feeding the hungry, visiting people in prison, and the like.

The man can't help himself and interrupts Jesus to point out that Jesus seems to be talking about work's righteousness. "You're saying," he declares to Jesus, "she's earned her way into heaven?"

"No," replied Jesus. "I *am* not saying that at all. I *am* saying that I *am* the way, not you, not your church, not your reading of John's gospel, and not the claim of any individual Christian or particular congregation. I *am* making the determination, and it is by my grace that anyone gets in, including you. Do you want to argue?"[31]

The man didn't, of course, and, I suspect, neither does any of us.

CHAPTER EIGHT

Heaven, Hell, the Ascension, and the Second Coming of Jesus

WITHIN CHRISTIANITY HEAVEN, hell, the ascension, and the second coming of Jesus are usually part of any discussion of salvation. The church has taught that being "saved" means going to heaven, being "lost" means going to hell. Jesus, who ascended to the right hand of God, the church has also said, will return again, initiating the events of the last days.

The preeminent church historian, Martin Marty, once wrote about hell (a subject that touches on all the rest):

> *The question of hell relates to the theme of divine judgment, "the wrath of God," the calling to account and the like. Loading up those themes with this glamorous, colorful, mythosymbolic, ever-changing (also within the canonical scriptures) envisioning, so subject to caricature and so useful to terrifying children, does not advance belief in the God revealed as a God of love.[32]*

Never mind Marty's wise warning, some Christians are fascinated with the prospects of a bad end for those who do not accept Jesus. *The Left Behind* series of novels about the last days on earth, by Tim LaHaye and Jerry Jenkins (2008), sold more than sixty million books. Obviously more than a few Christians have been drawn to this story about the end time, and specifically about the "Rapture," that point in history when Jesus returns to gather the faithful to himself and leaves behind the damned. I suspect most readers do not consider themselves as being among the ones to be left behind. Some of them may believe they know people who will be. All of them obviously consider the notion of Jesus floating down from heaven on a cloud signaling the beginning of the end of life on earth as a real possibility, if not a certainty.

While laity bought the books by the thousands, there was immediate criticism from mainline scholars who minced no words in debunking the notion that the "Rapture" is biblical. But the damage was done. Record-breaking sales created the impression that the vast majority of Christians believe Jesus will come back to exact retribution on the unrighteous. But surveys raise doubts as to whether this is in fact something a broad spectrum of Christians truly believe. According to the Pew survey mentioned earlier, 74 percent of Christians believe in heaven, but only 59 percent believe in hell. "Belief in hell, where people who have led bad lives and die without repenting are eternally punished," concludes the report, "is less common than is belief in life after death or heaven. In every religious tradition, including all the Christian traditions, belief in hell is at least slightly less prevalent than belief in heaven."[33]

A NEW HEAVEN AND A NEW HELL

I find little comfort in the percentage difference between people who believe in heaven and those who believe in hell when the latter make up 59 percent of those asked. On the other hand, like most surveys, the specifics are lacking that could help us better understand what the percentages actually mean. For example, we don't know what people mean by "heaven" or "hell." We know that when people say they believe in God, they may be referring to a power, spirit, higher consciousness, or something else quite removed from the biblical concept of a Creator God who is personal. The same diversity of specifics might exist in regard to heaven and hell. Is heaven some kind of paradise? Is hell a pit of fire? Is either a "place," or a state of being? These questions are left unanswered by the survey results. The percentages about belief in heaven and hell in other surveys have actually been considerably higher than those in the Pew survey.[34]

One conclusion I draw from reading these kinds of surveys is that sacred texts have a mixed influence on beliefs. As I have said, in general people believe what they believe, whether it is what their tradition teaches or not. The majority of religious people think for themselves in spite of the public perception that most accept what they are told without questioning it. I think this is especially true in regard to heaven, hell, and the second coming of Jesus. In part this may be because no one knows anything for sure about any of it, even the writers of the Bible. The future is just that, the future, and life has taught us that it often turns out to be different from what we think. Matters of faith are no more predictable than anything else.

Yet some Christian thinkers are troubled by the spectrum of beliefs about heaven and hell. A series of articles on hell in *The Christian Century* magazine[35] showed significant diversity in views on hell (and heaven), but surprisingly, all the writers considered it an essential theological concept for Christians not to lose. One writer suggested hell was important to slow down the church's movement toward an easy universalism. Another said hell was a non-negotiable item of Christian vocabulary because of its scriptural roots, creedal tradition, and being a staple of Christian preaching and art for centuries. What's more, he said, the substance of heaven and salvation is emptied of meaning if not contrasted with the reality of the finality of separation from God that hell represents. Another insisted that the hope seen in Jesus' post-crucifixion descent into hell affirms a belief that nothing is out of reach of God, but only if one has experienced hell and met Jesus in it. Another was confident that hell was integral to the gospel because there would be no need of a savior unless there was something to be saved from, i.e., hell. If we believe in Jesus, she went on to say, keep his commandments, and desire his return, we can be assured that we will—like those he met in hell—see him coming to bring us into his heavenly glory. Yet another writer argued that as tempting as it is to give up hell, it is in fact a Christian distinctive, and that giving it up would result in heaven being dimmed down. Two others also argued for hell, one saying that it serves as a witness to the seriousness with which Jesus Christ enters into solidarity with the poor and disenfranchised; the other suggesting hell is a metaphor for the evil of this world that, when seen clearly, compels one to participate in the pain and suffering it causes.

I read each of these brief essays and found myself remarkably unmoved by them, and more than a little frustrated by how utterly out of touch they are with where most church members live. I decided to see if the response of church members was different from mine, so I asked several lay people to review the articles. Their response in fact paralleled mine. They found most of what was written to be obtuse, little more than theological gibberish—with one notable exception. It was the historian among the eight, the venerable Martin Marty quoted above, whose piece spoke to them. They understood him to say that hell as taught and preached is a poor excuse for soliciting conversion, especially among children, hardly worthy of the gospel of love.

I think the reaction of these lay people represents what most Christians who might read the article would say. Heaven and hell are not concepts they think about a lot, and hardly ever in the traditional way that some of these scholars described hell. But this doesn't mean either has no place in their vocabulary or their

Christian commitment, only that they need a way to think about a new heaven and a new earth that makes sense to them.

I believe the resurrection opens the door to just that. It is the context for understanding heaven and hell. The latter represents the denial of the future that is unfolding while the former affirms it. When Jesus talked of the coming kingdom or reign of God, and as we pray, "Your kingdom come, your will be done, on earth as it is in heaven," he and we are talking about the unfolding of God's future, a future captured in the vision of the end of time marked by a new heaven and a new earth (Revelation 21:1-5). Heaven is to participate in this re-creation of creation itself, this redemption of the whole world that is coming. Hell is to live under the illusion that there is no heaven, only earth. It is to consciously ignore a will greater than your own. It rejects the connectedness of all life. Hell is to believe that what is *is* all there is.

This necessarily closes the door to a conscious relationship with the divine. The effect this has is to close off any path that can lead us to experience forgiveness for the pain, hurt, and suffering we may have caused others. It is not impossible, but certainly difficult, to forgive ourselves when there is no one to ask forgiveness from. One important dimension of believing in God is that we can do that with God. We can ask for forgiveness from God because we can trust in an unconditional divine love that always forgives. That experience increases the chance that we can find the courage to forgive ourselves for wrongs done to others. Being conscious of those wrongs without any road to forgiveness being possible is hell. To know God forgives invites us not to withhold it from ourselves. Living with the consciousness of unforgiven wrongs is what hell is; it is in the deepest sense what Christian theology has called alienation. What's more, if there is life after death, then it stands to reason that the living hell we create for ourselves in this life follows us into the next.

But faith in God saves us from that hell, now and forever, and that is what we call heaven. The reason Christians believe in heaven is the same reason we believe in the resurrection of Jesus. We believe in the God of all creation who made heaven and earth, and who dwells in heaven and earth, because heaven and earth are in the deepest sense one. Our awareness of this reality is the beginning of a new creation in and through us, just as the Apostle Paul described it (2 Corinthians 5:17). Once you get this truth deep inside, you become a different person, a person who becomes an agent of reconciliation in the flesh (5:19), who by virtue of being who you are becomes an ambassador for the good news God has given to the world in Jesus' resurrection (5:21). To believe, then, is to begin living in a new realm appropriately called "heaven" (*ouranos*), or the abode of God. Not to believe is to live outside the abode of God, the presence of God. Hell is to be limited to the old order that is passing away. It can be appropriately described as being out of touch with the real world.

Jesus' resurrection was an earthly event, a here and now birth of new life. We can now see why the *bodily* resurrection is the point. Neither the gospel writers nor Paul meant that Jesus' soul was transported to a realm to which no one else is privy. They were talking about his having a new body. He had become a new creation, similar to the old, yet altogether different. To believe in the bodily resurrection is to believe in the goodness of flesh and blood, made and re-made as creations of God.

THE ASCENSION

The ascension of Jesus is not about Jesus shooting up into the universe, but is the biblical way of saying the new creation has begun, though not yet fully manifest. It is the "here, but not yet" concept theologians discuss in regard to the end of time.[36] The reign of God has begun, but it is not yet completed. How long it will be in becoming complete is a question based on time and space, yet unknown, because a thousand years is but a day to God and a day is like a thousand years (2 Peter 3:8).

Actually, the words of the angel to the disciples in the ascension story in Acts are the key to its meaning:

> *While he was going and they were gazing up toward heaven, suddenly two men in white robes stood by them. They said, "Men of Galilee, why do you stand looking up toward heaven? This Jesus, who has been taken up from you into heaven, will come in the same way as you saw him go into heaven (Acts 1:10-11).*

Luke also includes the story of the Ascension in his gospel (24:50-53), which is virtually the same as in Acts with some differences. There is no angel in the gospel account. Jesus "withdraws" from them and goes into heaven, but the text does not say the disciples "see" this happen. They then return to Jerusalem rejoicing and being Temple observant. The details in the Acts text are more extensive. It says that an angel speaks to the disciples as Jesus "was lifted up, and a cloud took him out of their sight" v. 9), telling them not to stand there looking into the heavens because Jesus would someday return as he had gone away.

In the New Testament worldview, heaven was up. It was natural that Luke would describe the time when Jesus was no longer seen by his disciples as his having gone up to heaven. The fact that we do not share their worldview does not mean we have to reject the message Acts conveys—the Jesus they knew who was crucified and raised from the dead had been with them in the flesh again in order to assure them that God was indeed doing a new thing in him (Isaiah 43:19). Unfortunately those Christians who insist in literalizing the language reflecting a pre-modern view of the universe are sacrificing the message in this text in the process.

The disciples, on the other hand, got the message, returned to Jerusalem, and started praying and preaching about the raised Jesus who was and is God's initiation of a new age. But even as Jesus was the new beginning, he was at the same time a fulfillment and confirmation of God's claim on Israel. In him Israel's call to be a blessing to all nations (Genesis 12:3) was made flesh and blood. Paul's mission to the Gentiles rightly picked up on this vocation. Israel's covenant with God was not nullified in Jesus. It was reaffirmed—ratified, if you will. Christians have mistakenly sought to make Jesus unique by severing him from Judaism, when the New Testament sets him firmly in it. This is seen quite clearly in the Greek concept of the immortality of the soul, which stands in marked contrast to what both Judaism and early Christianity understood about resurrection. Having removed the body from Jesus' resurrection, it was predictable that the church would make the ascension, heaven, hell, and the second coming "other-worldly" events that rescued people from their earthly existence or condemned them to damnation in a world also removed from earthly existence.

Many Christians are uncomfortable with the concepts of heaven and hell, and perhaps the ascension, precisely because they reject an ancient worldview without realizing that it is unnecessary to reject the messages couched in ancient images. If it is possible to believe Jesus was raised from the dead, it is no less plausible to suggest he made himself known to his disciples for a while in order to convince them that the new age he inaugurated had in fact begun. Once they believed this to be true, his visible presence was no longer necessary. The ascension is the story of that moment. The second coming is the belief that he will one day make himself visible again. Heaven is the faith that this is true. Hell is choosing to limit one's trust in that which is seen.

Being a person of faith does not mean living in a fantasy world, nor is speaking of such things as heaven and hell, the ascension, or the second coming a sign that one rejects modern science. Faith is a way of seeing the world without limiting what you believe to what you see. If we can believe the mystical connection between a parent and child is real even though we cannot "see" it or prove it exists, so believing in God—who cannot be "seen"—makes it possible to trust that life is more than what is observable. Thus, the wisdom of the writer of Hebrews is affirmed. Faith is in truth "the assurance of things hoped for, the conviction of things not seen" (11:1).

THE SECOND COMING

It has been said that the second coming of Jesus arose out of the disciples' disappointment over the first one. He just didn't perform up to messianic expectations. Israel's kingdom was not restored, the age of peace didn't dawn, and foreign domination of Jerusalem did not end. Others have speculated that the coming of the Holy Spirit at Pentecost was the second coming. Jesus told his disciples God would send the Comforter, who would cause them to remember what he had said to them (John 14:26). For these Christians his promise was fulfilled on Pentecost. Still others believe the second coming will signal the end of time and the coming judgment of God on all who are unrighteous. Writers like LaHaye and Jenkins believe this will be initiated by the "Rapture."

None of these views appeals to a large cross section of Christians, which is why so many Christians think very little about the second coming or do not put much stock in it. But something important is lost as a result of this indifference. I have become convinced that the importance of believing in the second coming is not because of what will happen in the future. Rather, it is because of what that belief should lead us to do now.

I do not believe the New Testament writers were disappointed in Jesus' first appearing and made up the story of his second coming to fill the void. The gospels and the development of the church emerged for precisely the opposite reason. His resurrection inspired them to preach and teach that he was the One for whom Jews had been waiting, the Anointed One, through whom God was inaugurating a new day, new world, new creation. Their own tradition included the story of the Flood that spoke of God's power to re-create a fallen creation. Israel was yet another sign of this divine engagement with humanity. The New Testament says that Jesus was yet another. The New Testament is a witness to the belief that the emergence of the Jesus movement that became the church was still another sign.

In the context of their strong convictions, the followers of Jesus spoke of a second coming as a completion of what God initiated in Jesus. They believed there would be an end to history as they knew it, but not, as so many believe today, an end to earth. The New Testament is grounded in the here and now. Where this message becomes convoluted is in The Book of Revelation. Even though it speaks of heaven and earth merging into a new Jerusalem (Revelation 21) here on earth, it also contains apocalyptic images of a judgment where God reigns hell down on unbelievers. Here less-trained interpreters seem to have won the day in convincing many Christians that Revelation is about an end time to come, when the best scholarship shows that it was a book written out of and, at the same time, for the Christian community in the latter half of the first century.

That said, the second coming of Jesus was, I believe, central to the early church envisioning God's new creation becoming a reality here on earth. Jesus, then, was not returning to punish. He was returning to signal the power of God's grace restoring the whole of creation to its rightful order.

Apparently some Christians in Thessalonica took this to mean they should sit and wait for this great event to happen. Paul wrote to them and said the opposite was true (2 Thessalonians 3:6-13), that this hope of Jesus' return was sufficient reason to work to make all things new. Feeding the hungry, clothing the naked, and caring for the sick and the imprisoned were signs that God's kingdom was already coming on earth. The social gospel is not an obligation for Christians waiting for the end to come. It is a witness to the content of the new beginning rising up from the end of what has been. Peace and justice *on earth* are coming, and the household of God will include all who do the will of God, regardless of the religious label they wear. Lions and lambs will lie down together.

The key word for what the New Testament is saying about the

second coming of Jesus is "proleptic." It means "the representation or assumption of a future act or development as if presently existing or accomplished."[37] The New Testament witness is about the future beginning now. The phrase "heaven on earth" is a helpful way to express this belief because heaven and earth are moving toward a single reality. The two will become one, and the work that Christians do now becomes all the more important as part of this coming reality.

Yet I am not so naïve as to think this kind of imagery is easy for people to believe, or actually pay much attention to. Nor does it help that when administering the sacrament of Communion, ministers often misquote the Apostle Paul saying in his account of the Lord's Supper: "For as often as you eat this bread and drink the cup, you proclaim the Lord's death until he comes again."

The problem is that the text does not say those words, and the difference is significant. What Paul actually says is this: "For as often as you eat this bread and drink the cup, you proclaim the Lord's death *until he comes*" (1 Corinthians 11:26). The Greek word for "come" used here (*erchomai*) can suggest the conditional "may come," but it does not mean "come again." Yet this is often what congregations hear clergy say. Although perhaps not intentional, it turns out to be very misleading, tying the act of Communion with the misunderstood belief that history is waiting for Jesus to return, when the text suggests the opposite, that Jesus comes in the here and now every time his followers share in the act of Communion.

This text also reflects the urgency of the early church to preach about Jesus in word and deed, which was born of its conviction that the future had begun to unfold in Jesus and was continuing through the church. The first Christians were grounded in human relationships and human endeavors, not in spite of their hopes for the future, but because of their expectation that Jesus would return in the full glory of God's new creation. As such, the hope of a "second coming" simply added meaning to the first.

CHAPTER NINE

A Jesus to Believe In

AT LONG LAST, then, a human Jesus to believe in. Or so I thought. Then I met with an evangelical leader who asked me, "If Christianity is not the only way, then why be a Christian?"

It was a sincere question. I gave him a sincere answer. God raised Jesus from the dead. This is what makes Jesus distinctive. In that act God was saying that life conquers death, good is stronger than evil, and the God/human relationship will not be broken. This "word" God spoke in Jesus' resurrection impacts the world, not just Christians. It is the new thing Isaiah said God would do (43:19). It is the new creation John's Revelation describes.

But his question was off the mark for two important reasons. The first is that in good faith his question reflected the tendency for Christians who do not embrace substitutionary atonement nonetheless to cling to it in one form or another. But my argument is that Jesus can be central to our faith as Christians without his death being the means of forgiveness and salvation. I would even go so far as to say that Jesus' resurrection is an act of atonement in that by raising Jesus God declared once and for all that humanity is forgiven, and futher, that the human and the divine are and forever will be "at-one-ment." In other words, the resurrection is the only atonement needed or possible in the context of unconditional grace and love.

The second reason I think this evangelical leader's question missed the mark is because distinctiveness is not the point of Jesus. Who he was—and is—certainly marks his life as critical in human history, but his distinctiveness lies in the fact that God chose to raise him from the dead. Why Jesus? is a question I will address in a moment. Here the point is that Jesus was the human instrument God used to fulfill the promise to Abraham that through his descendants all the world would be blessed by raising him from the dead. It cannot be overstated that we who are called Christians follow Jesus because God did not allow his death to be the last word, but raised him to life again. Without the empty tomb, it is unlikely that anyone would be discussing the meaning of his death. More likely is that Jesus would have been lost in history.

It seems so obvious to me now (but it has not always been so) that Jesus did not have to be divine for us to focus on the resurrection. There is no need for a doctrine of the incarnation.[38] On the contrary, in the light of the resurrection it was his humanity that made his life so compelling. Jesus did not anoint himself with the power of the Holy Spirit. It would seem that whatever the early Christians believed about Jesus being divine, it did not include that he was different in kind from the rest of humanity. God was the One who did the declaring, just as God was the One who did the raising from the dead. In the life of Jesus, God was God and Jesus was Jesus. This is the starting point for meeting a Jesus we can believe in.

Seeing Jesus as the man he was confirms he was of flesh and blood, subject to physical death as are all other human beings. This is our point of identity with him. He lived and breathed as we do. If he had not, nothing he said and did would be real. His words and deeds would lose meaning because they would have been extensions of God being God. What else would we expect but power over nature, wisdom that confounds mere mortals, and actions expressing divine control.

The church has said that Jesus was a man, suffering as we do in all ways, but did not sin, while also insisting that he was God. This does not represent a paradox of faith. It is a contradiction. The idea that Jesus had to be both human and divine for God to relate to the people and the people to relate to God simply makes no sense. If Jesus was God, then he was not human. Saying he was God is not a small thing. It is a very huge thing, but not for the reasons the church has said. As God, his life becomes a drama no more real than a Broadway play. Human response to the gospel stories is something like a theater audience, moved by emotions created by what turns out not to be real. This is a modern expression of Docetism (the belief that Jesus was not truly human), which ironically the church rejected outright.

The value of seeing divinity as the biblical way to speak of Jesus' intimate relationship with God as a man is that it provides us with a point of identity with him and at the same time makes his resurrection more believable. Just as Jesus did not pray to himself, Jesus did not raise himself. In this way, his humanity invites us to reframe the question about Jesus' relationship to God. Rather than saying Jesus was God, it makes more sense to ask if we can trust that God is *like* the man Jesus. We have already emphasized that if Jesus was God, then Christianity is right in claiming that it triumphs over Judaism, Islam, and all other religions. We may respect other religions, but in the final analysis we believe those who follow these paths must someday come to follow Jesus or be rejected by God.

The Christians I know would not say it in such a judgmental way, but what they believe inevitably leads to this conclusion. That is because this kind of triumphal attitude cannot be avoided unless and until Christianity stops insisting Jesus was God and that he died for our sins. The belief that God is *like* Jesus is a much more inclusive way to frame the relationship. It focuses on the efficacy of Christian claims in understanding God rather than counteracting the claims of other faiths. Following Jesus takes on the meaning of stepping onto a path that trusts that the things Jesus said and did reveal something of the mind and heart of God, a claim that is both reasonable and nonexclusive. Jesus doesn't have to be the only way to know what God is like.

The practical impact on many Christians who hear the church's message that they must believe Jesus was God is that they are no longer sure if they can call themselves a Christian. This is an unnecessary choice forced upon them. You can affirm Jesus as a man and also affirm he was raised from the dead. He then becomes someone you can believe in because his humanity makes sense. His life was given over to God. His will was to do God's will. His way was to follow God's way. His actions showed God's compassion. His trust in God's goodness and power is the example for us to follow. This is the Jesus beyond the church's doctrines and creeds. It is, I believe, the Jesus the world can and will take seriously, if the church has the courage to preach and teach about him, and then make him known in its own attitudes and actions.

JESUS AND THE VIRGIN BIRTH

If Jesus was a man just like other men, what about the virgin birth? It is an important question. Two of the four gospels— Matthew 1:18-25 and Luke 1:26-38—contain virgin birth stories. It is significant, though, that Mark and John do not. Neither apparently considered the story essential to the narratives they were telling about Jesus' life, death, and resurrection. Nor did Paul, since he does not mention the virgin birth story either.

The fact that Jesus himself never mentions anything related to being born of a virgin—or anything at all about his birth, for that matter—suggests Mark, John, and Paul may have been right. The virgin birth story does not add to Jesus' significance. What's more,

A Different Jesus

virgin birth stories were common in the ancient world, and are also found in other religious traditions.[39] So for Jesus to have been born of a virgin would not have made his birth more notable to the people of his day. This suggests we should look for some other reason for Matthew and Luke telling these stories. Indeed, we do not have to look very far.

In Matthew the story of Jesus' birth and King Herod's efforts to kill the infant Jesus serves as a way to underscore for later generations that from his birth Jesus was seen as a threat to Roman authority. This point was reinforced by the fact that non-Jewish astrologers (the three Magi) were the ones who brought Herod the news that another king was born. In other words, the perceived threat that Jesus' birth represented to Rome was recognized beyond the limited world of Judaism.

The message Luke intended to convey through his virgin birth story is best understood in the context of his having written Acts. The Pentecost story in Acts 2:1-13 says that the church emerged because the disciples were filled with the Holy Spirit, just as Jesus had emerged because Mary was made pregnant by the Holy Spirit. Perhaps Luke intended the parallel we can see in the two stories? The birth of Jesus and the birth of the church were acts of God, not the result of human effort.[40]

At the very least we can say that Matthew's and Luke's virgin birth stories were just that—stories—but with theological significance, which Mark and John were able to define in their own way without using these kinds of stories. This is important because once Christian theology separates itself from the need for Jesus to have died for the sins of the world, his life becomes all the more compelling because he was the man he was, fully human, not needing to be divine to be an instrument of God here on earth.

WHY JESUS?

Why was he raised? Why not someone else before or after him? Why this particular man?

It is an excellent question, but without a definitive answer. My approach to it is similar to the question: "Why the Jews?" Why Abraham? Why the Hebrews? Why Moses? These are question the Talmud itself raises and seeks to answer—but without any consensus. The reason is that there is no final answer. It is in the last analysis speculative. But that doesn't mean the Jews were not chosen or that Jesus was not raised from the dead.

It is clearly the case that the sense of election among Jews exists. The tradition is real. No one knows its origins, but that it exists is not in question. What matters is its meaning. Speculation about why it exists can be an interesting endeavor, but the meaning and purpose of election is quite separate from all of that.

I believe the same principle applies to the question of why Jesus? The experience and testimony of millions is that he was raised. Why it turned out to be him and not someone else does not change or alter the fact that his name is the one associated with this transformative event.

So why Jesus? There is no final answer. But that it was Jesus is supported by the testimony of those who experienced it and then passed it down to every generation since. Do we wish for a more satisfying answer? Yes, of course. But is our faith dependent upon it. No, not in the least.

JESUS' CROSS AND OURS

To say Jesus didn't die for our sins does not mean his death didn't matter. Quite the opposite. Seeing Jesus as the man he was means we cannot and should not avoid the harsh reality of his cross. If Jesus didn't die for our sins, he did die because of sin. His death was an injustice, leaving his blood on the hands of people who followed fear and hate instead of love. This unjust act was contradicted by Jesus doing just the opposite, giving everything he was to the ethic of love and to the prophetic ministry that love compelled him to follow.

The absence of love as the dominant ethic of the world is why his crucifixion serves as a symbol for what faces anyone today who chooses love over fear, compassion over power. Death and destruction are the by-products of hate. Injustice is the by-product of the abuse of power and position. Poverty is the by-product of materialism. And on it goes. The cross represents the human choice to say "no" to it all. Jesus did not have to go to Jerusalem. It was a choice he made because any other choice would have betrayed his commitment to doing the will of God in the service of love and justice.

To follow the man Jesus means we will face the same choice. As one of my teachers often said, "No one should claim the cross as a symbol of Jesus' sacrifice without also claiming it as a sign of one's own lifestyle. Jesus the man went to the cross, and this same Jesus calls us to be willing to do the same thing. "If any want to become my followers," he said, "let them deny themselves and take up their cross and follow me" (Mark 8:34).

I think Jesus is saying that being willing to choose the way of the cross is a prerequisite to "followship." This is the case because the cross is an indictment of a world turned away from God, a world convinced that earthly power, whether religious or political, is the final authority. To follow the man Jesus is a commitment to accepting whatever risk or threat the ethic of love may involve.

But why would anyone make this commitment if Jesus was not uniquely God, not uniquely divine, but human just as we are? In all candor, a significant part of the answer is family and cultural context. While people usually claim faith for themselves as adults, if at all, the family and cultural context in which they were raised has an enormous impact on what faith they claim or reject. A child raised in a Christian home will be formed in the Christian tradition, as will a Jewish or Muslim child. A child raised in an irreligious family context will be influenced by that. If the larger social context is predominantly Christian, Jewish, Muslim, or secular, that will reinforce what is learned in the home or provide a contrast that will impact faith formation positively or negatively. So the answer to the question, "Why be a Christian, why follow Jesus?" is in part shaped by the happenstance of a person's birth.

But the choice to have faith as an adult is also influenced by the tradition itself. Here the life and teachings of Jesus, and even more, the way of Jesus, become a significant factor. According to the four New Testament gospels, Jesus taught that God will be the first priority in the life of anyone who chooses to do the will of God. The way he said a person shows devotion to God is with neighborly love, with justice, and with showing mercy and forgiveness.

It is, I think, easy to underestimate the attracting power of unconditional love. But in the person of Jesus it was captivating to many people who lived when he lived, and has become the foundation for millions since. In some respects this points to the essential role the church plays in how people respond to Jesus. Jesus being taken seriously as a model of living a life devoted to God depends in no small degree on how well the church embodies the life and teachings of Jesus. This is a subject too large for this context, but its importance needs to be highlighted here for future exploration. It comes down to this. The church's faithfulness in following Jesus' call to a singular devotion to God, unconditional love of neighbor, and the practice of peace and justice in the world influences those who struggle with having faith and/or what kind of faith to have.

Seeing Jesus as a man and not God, then, is a theological argument with practical consequences—one social, the other theological. But the key is Jesus being human, not divine. Understanding the cross as a sign of the cost we must pay for committing ourselves to the ethic of love is the message for us in our own time in history. If Jesus was God, that challenge seems beyond us as mere humans. But if he was human as we are, his death becomes the true example of the kind of commitment to sacrificial love we are also called to embody. The irony is that shifting our focus away from the cross to the resurrection is the key to claiming the power of the cross for our own lives.

That, I believe, is a Christian theology that is big enough for the religiously plural world we live in, and the most winsome witness to Jesus the Christian community can make.

THE JESUS CONNECTION

But there is something more.

In John 15:1-5, Jesus uses a vine/branch metaphor to describe the relationship he envisions between him and his disciples. In an earlier book, I argued that Christians today would do well to take this metaphor seriously because it underscores the mystical union not only possible between us and Jesus, but also necessary if we are to have the courage and power to remain faithful to our call to ministry.[41]

The resurrection is the basis for any of this being possible. If Jesus was not raised, our relationship with him remains only a matter of trying to follow his teachings, in the same way followers of other religious teachers do. But his being raised from the dead changed everything. His disciples experienced his presence, not just remembered his teachings. Based on what Jesus says in John 15, sensing his presence should not only be possible, but should not be altogether unexpected. John includes other texts that support this point of faith. In John 10:30, Jesus speaks of being "one" with God and then later prays that his disciples would experience a similar "oneness" with each other (John 17:22).

This "oneness" with God and with the living presence of Jesus goes to the heart of the entire contemplative movement within Christianity, rooted, of course, in the monastic tradition that has produced some of the great saints of the church. Just as the argument for the resurrection of Jesus has reason to support it, yet goes beyond it, so, too, does the possibility of experiencing a mystical union with the living Jesus.

Through the years I have led weekend silent retreats for people of all ages, from college students to seniors. I always told them just before the silence begins to trust that the Holy Spirit would bring them not so much what they wanted, but what they needed. It is in such a context that mystical experience has shown itself again and again to be real and trustworthy. Retreat members have often spoken of having moments during the weekend when they felt strongly they were not alone. They often described the experience using the words of faith that they sensed the presence of Jesus.

I believe the resurrection is why their experience should not be dismissed as some sort of illusion, if not delusion. If Jesus was raised, anything is possible, that with God all things are possible. Jesus was raised. That is the Christian story.

ENDNOTES

1 John A. T. Robinson, *Honest To God* (Philadelphia: Westminster Press, 1963), p. 28.

2 A Pew Research Center in 2008 found the following: 70 percent of American Christians say there is more than one way to eternal life, i.e., salvation, including 57 percent of evangelicals, 79 percent of Catholics, and 83 percent of mainline Protestants. See its report on American religious attitudes entitled "Religion in America: Non-Dogmatic, Diverse and Politically Relevant Religious Beliefs & Practices, Social & Political Views," Report 2, June 23, 2008.

3 Amy-Jill Levine and Douglas Knight, "Biblical Views of God," Blog at the *Huffington Post*, November 19, 2011.

4 Joan Chittister, *Called to Question: A Spiritual Memoir* (NY: Sheed & Ward, 2004), p. 2.

5 Some might say *modus tollens* is how you prove a negative because it "denies the consequent," such as "If A, then B. Not A, then not B." But I would argue *modus tollens* does not apply to the case for God because "not A" cannot be shown to be true.

6 Levine, Knight "Biblical Views of God."

7 Reported in the *Minneapolis Star Tribune*, Friday, January 31, 2014, Life Style section.

8 E. J. Montini, "Is Football Worth It?" posted November 12, 2013.

9 Scott McKnight, *A Community Called Atonement* (Nashville: Abingdon Press, 2007), p. 1. McKnight's approach to the issue of atonement differs from others in that his concern is whether or not atonement works. That is, does it "redeem" people, change them, make them more likely to live by the ethic of love? He says this is possible only if atonement creates an atoning community, and an atoning community thrives on the message of atonement. In short, McKnight believes individual atonement cannot be separated from community of atonement.

10 There is no single atonement theory, but the four basic ones are as follows: The ransom theory (Christus Victor), which says that Jesus' death was the ransom God paid to Satan to reclaim humanity; the satisfaction theory (St. Anselm), which says Jesus was a substitute for humanity and

97

paid the price for us for the forgiveness of sin; the penal substitution theory (Calvin), which says Jesus' death met the requirement for justice by God, who was offended by humanity's sin; and the moral influence theory, which interprets Jesus' death as an example of faithfulness so winsome that it would win back humanity to God. The most recent, called "scapegoat" atonement, proposed by anthropologist René Girard. From his perspective the human desire for what others have, what he called "mimetic desire," leads to violence. The pervasiveness of violence led to societies finding others, often an innocent person, to blame for their own violence or "sins." The "innocent" was deemed guilty, the society innocent. The collective human need for a scapegoat, Girard says, was reversed in Jesus as the Son of God. He was innocent. Humanity was guilty. But his innocent suffering was God's way of entering into human life to become the ultimate scapegoat for humanity on the cross, eliminating any further need for a scapegoat or sacrifice for human evil, the "sacrifice to end all sacrifice," as it has been described.

11 Most Christians do not make the distinction between substitutionary or penal atonement, but Derek Flood rightly argues that they are not at all the same, a mistake often made by scholars. He says substitutionary atonement should be understood within the biblical model of "restorative justice," wherein salvation means the wound caused by sin. This restorative justice model is the basis upon which Flood draws on Gustaf Aulen's *Christus Victor* to underscore the theme of evil being defeated in the death of Jesus. He rejects the penal atonement for many reasons, not least because, he says, its insistence on understanding sin only in terms of "legal acquittal" ignores the restorative dimension rooted in scripture. His books argues that restoration is the central plotline of the New Testament and provides the key to understanding the meaning of divine justice. See Derek Flood, *Healing the Gospel: A Radical Vision of Grace, Justice, and the Cross* (Eugene, Ore, Cascade Books, an imprint of Wipf and Stock Publishers), 2012.

12 Mark Heim's book on atonement, *Saved from Sacrifice: A Theology of the Cross* (Grand Rapids: Eerdmans, 2006), p. 4. Heim's book draws heavily on Girard's scapegoat theory, which he sees as the key to reclaiming a viable atonement theology.

13 Craig Evans, *Fabricating Jesus: How Modern Scholars Distort the Gospels* (Downers Grover: IVP, 2006), (op. cit.), p. 192. Further, New Testament scholar Craig Evans insists this is the fundamental claim of the New Testament itself: "Jesus is Savior of Jews and non-Jews alike, primarily because of the atoning value of his death on the cross. In short, by dying on the cross, Jesus paid for the sins of humanity. This is the teaching of all of Christianity's earliest teachers and writers. Not every New Testament

writing speaks to this topic, of course, but most do, and not one suggests an alternative understanding of Jesus' death," p. 97.

14   Heim suggests that when we speak of Jesus dying for our sins we should mean that we stand with Christ's saving work to unveil and overturn "scapegoat violence." *Saved from Sacrifice* (op, cit.), p. 254.

15   For a fuller discussion of the pre-Christian belief of a messiah who would suffer and die to make atonement for Israel and for the world, see N. T. Wright, *Jesus and the Victory of God* (Minneapolis: Fortress Press, 1996), pp. 584–92.

16   Amy-Jill Levine, The Misunderstood Jew: *The Church and the Scandal of the Jewish Jesus* (HarperSanFrancisco, 2006), p. 200.

17   Ibid., pp. 200–10.

18   From an unpublished paper that was the Prologue to Incomplete Book Manuscript that Goetz did not live to complete. Based on the Prologue and this focus on atonement during his academic career, Goetz's work marked a radical departure from both traditional and contemporary atonement theories in arguing that Jesus' death atoned not only for humanity's but atoned for God's responsibility for unmerited suffering. The Prologue is both profound and intriguing in what it promised, but, alas, never came to be. It can be accessed at www.ronaldgoetz.com.

19   Amy-Jill Levine says some rabbis argue that Isaac was actually killed only to reappear again. See her lectures 5 and 6, disc 3, in The Great Courses series entitled "The Old Testament." For more information go to www. thegreatcourses.com.

20   Wright, *Jesus and the Victory of God* (op. cit.), p. 592.

21   The Rev. Dr. Craig Watts (op. cit.), Senior Minister, Royal Palms Christian Church, Coral Gables, Florida, and a close friend, critiqued this passage with such clarity and conciseness that I include his comments here to underscore both the importance of and difficulties posed by Trinitarian thinking. "Jan, you are right that there is no explicit doctrine of the Trinity in the New Testament but the worship of Jesus found even in pre-Pauline strains of the scripture and the worship of Jesus in Gospel narratives, like the resurrection account in Matthew and elsewhere de-manded the church give some sort of account the would lead in the direction of Binitarianism if not Trinitarianism. It is important, I believe, that Jesus when confronting the Tempter, refused him worship, he cited from scripture, 'Worship the Lord your God and serve only him' (Matt 4:10, Luke 4:8). When Cornelius fell at the feet of Peter and worshiped him, Peter objected, saying 'Stand up; I am only a mortal' (Acts 10:25-26). Again, when the people began to offer Paul and Barnabas worship, they stopped them, saying, 'We are mortals just like you' (Acts 14:11-15). In striking contrast, in every one of the stories in the Gospels where

we are told people 'worshiped him,' Jesus offered no hint of objection whatsoever. These things are part of the memory of the church that both sanctioned the explicit worship of Jesus and the development of Trinitarian theology. Without Trinitarianism, the worship of Jesus would have to be regarded as idolatry."

22 For a comprehensive argument for the historical reliability of the gospel accounts of the resurrection of Jesus, see N. T. Wright, *The Resurrection of the Son of God* (Minneapolis: Fortress Press, 2001).

23 Bart Erdman argues the depth of the disciples' grief made them prime candidates for hallucinatory visions. After all, he insists, people have hallucinations all the time, today and also at the time of Jesus. See his book, *How Jesus Became God: The Exaltation of a Jewish Preacher from Galilee* (San Francisco: HarperOne, 2014). For a response to his book by several scholars, see *How God Became Jesus: The Real Origins of Belief in Jesus' Divine Nature—A Response to Bart Ehrman* (Grand Rapids: Zondervan, 2014) by Michael F. Bird, Craig A. Evans, Simon Gathercole and Charles E. Hill.

24 For Marcus Borg and other scholars, while the gospel accounts of Jesus' resurrection may have actually been written by the writers and not added later (except for Mark 16:9ff), they reject any notion that there is a historical basis for the bodily resurrection of Jesus and is for practical purposes immaterial to the emergence of the church. This is like saying it doesn't matter if the disciples claimed something to be true that they knew wasn't. That would make the foundation for the church a hoax. Moreover, from this perspective, if Jesus' bodily remains were actually unearthed, which ironically film director James Cameron, in his 2007 documentary, *The Lost Tomb of Jesus,* implied had happened, it would have no impact on the faith of Christians.

I find such an argument astonishing, not unlike the notion that if life were to be found on another planet, Christians would simply stand and sing, "How Great Thou Art." Such a discovery would in fact bring into question everything Christians have been saying for centuries. The same can be said about finding the bones of Jesus. It would not matter only if what the church has taught since the first century did not matter. Even at that, to suggest that this news would not have an adverse impact on the Christian tradition is reductionism at its worst. The resurrection is the fundamental Christian claim. It is an enigma that anyone would suggest its factuality is inconsequential. This is not to say its importance makes it true, only that it is disingenuous to say it doesn't matter.

But let's reverse the skepticism. Does it actually make sense to believe that the resurrection didn't happen, that it was born out of the despair and fear that the New Testament itself says gripped the disciples, but which magically and inexplicably disappeared?

Does believing in the bodily resurrection of Jesus require more faith than supposing the Jesus movement within Judaism emerged in spite of the fact that the one they followed had been put to death? There is a presumption among many resurrection skeptics that reason is on their side, but only because there is no scientific evidence to support the claim that the human body can come back to life once it dies. Of course, there is no scientific evidence that God exists either, a crucial point to which we will devote the next chapter. Because science cannot account for something doesn't mean it didn't or cannot happen, as Princeton historian Elaine Pagels noted in an interview with Steve Paulson on Salon. When asked about the actual resurrection of Jesus, Professor Pagels suggested that a person can be a Christian and not believe in the actual bodily resurrection. This is something with which all open-minded Christians would agree. But when Paulson responded by saying, "It sounds like you're saying that it's perfectly possible to take the Bible very seriously, to be a Christian, and yet not to believe in the supernatural miracles that so many people simply cannot accept," she said, "Well, that may be. I don't dismiss all supernatural miracles, like a healing that can't be explained. Those do happen sometimes." She went on to say that a modern reading of the Bible does not require one to eliminate the supernatural from scripture altogether ("Gospel according to Judas" by Stephen Paulson, an interview with Elaine Pagels about the bitter quarrels among early Christians, why it's a bad idea to read the Bible literally, and the importance of this new discovery, posted April 2, 2007). That science does not explain all phenomena that occur or exist should be self-evident. So far as I am aware, there is no known reason for human beings to possess an appendix or tonsils, but we also know that both do in fact exist. In regard to the bodily resurrection of Jesus, the most science can say is that there is no known scientific evidence supporting it. It cannot say that such an event did not or cannot happen.

25 Bart Erdman argues the depth of the disciples' grief made them prime candidates for hallucinatory visions. *See How Jesus Became God: The Exaltation of a Jewish Preacher from Galilee* (San Francisco: HarperOne, 2014).

26 Here is where Derek Flood gets off the track. He insists that the resurrection must be connected to the incarnation. But to do so dilutes, if not undercuts, the resurrection. God did not need to be in Jesus in a unique way to raise Jesus from the dead. But I think Flood connects the incarnation and the resurrection precisely because he is trying to redeem the concept of atonement. It is an unnecessary, and I believe unwise theological move.

27 The Rev. Dr. Craig Watts (op. cit.). Senior Minister, Royal Palms Christian Church, Coral Gables, FL.

28 Levine, *The Misunderstood Jews* (op. cit.).

29 New Testament scholar, Larry Hurtado, has done extensive historical research on the question of when Jesus came to be seen as a divine figure by early Christians. He is convinced the evidence suggests this may have happened as early as 30-50 CE, and that it likely happened among Jewish Christians before the church becoming primarily Gentile or Roman. He also argues that this development represented a kind of new mutation or form of monotheism. In his comprehensive work on this subject, *Lord Jesus Christ: Devotion to Jesus in Earliest Christianity* (Grand Rapids: Eerdmans, 2003) Hurtado provides an in-depth analysis that suggests there was a conscious effort on the part of these Christians to maintain a monotheistic balance between Jesus and God "the Father." Careful not to assess the efficacy of such a belief, Hurtado also explores the influence this development of seeing Jesus as a divine figure had on future generations of Christians. A shorter version of this extensive volume can be found in his book, *How on Earth Did Jesus Become a God?: Historical Questions about Earliest Devotion to Jesus* (Grand Rapids: Eerdmans, 2005).

30 *Jesus and the Victory of God* (Minneapolis: Fortress, 1996), pp. 485–86.

31 Levine, T*he Misunderstood Jews* (op. cit.), pp. 92–93.

32 *The Christian Century*, June 3, 2008, p. 24.

33 The Pew Research Center survey report on American religious attitudes entitled "Religion in America: Non-Dogmatic, Diverse and Politically Relevant Religious Beliefs & Practices, Social & Political Views," Report 2, June 23, 2008 (op. cit. Endnote 6).

34 See http://www.religioustolerance.org/chr_poll3.htm#salv of the Ontario-based Consultants on Religious Tolerance.

35 *The Christian Century* (op. cit.)

36 The term used is "realized eschatology."

37 *Merriam-Webster* online dictionary.

38 See my criticism of Derek Flood connecting the incarnation with the resurrection in note #23.

39 Hinduism, Buddhism, Islam, and ancient Zoroastrianism all contain virgin birth and unusual birth stories.

40 This is the argument Charles Talbert makes about the meaning of Jesus' birth in his book, *Reading Luke: A Literary and Theological Commentary on the Third Gospel* (Macon, GA: Smith & Helwys Publishing, 2002), pp. 19–24.

41 See *The Jesus Connection: A Christian Spirituality* (St. Louis: Chalice Press, 1997).

OTHER BOOKS BY JAN G. LINN

How to Be an Open-Minded Christian without Losing Your Faith

What's Wrong with the Christian Right

Big Christianity: What's Right with the Religious Left

Rocking the Church Membership Boat:
  Counting Members or Having Members Who Count

Living Inside Out: Learning How to Pray the Serenity Prayer

22 Keys to Being a Minister (without Quitting
  or Wishing to Retire Early)

Reclaiming Evangelism: A Practical Guide for Mainline Churches

The Jesus Connection: A Christian Spirituality

What Church Members Wish Ministers Knew

Disciples: Reclaiming Our Identity, Reforming Our Practice
(co-authored with Michael Kinnamon)

What Ministers Wish Church Members Knew

Living Out God's Love

Christians Must Choose